Cold Calling

The Path to Fearless, Effective Cold Calling

(Learn Call Sales Strategies to Get New Clients and Sell)

Daniel Bowles

Published By **Zoe Lawson**

Daniel Bowles

All Rights Reserved

Cold Calling: The Path to Fearless, Effective Cold Calling (Learn Call Sales Strategies to Get New Clients and Sell)

ISBN 978-1-77485-663-5

No part of this guidebook shall be reproduced in any form without permission in writing from the publisher except in the case of brief quotations embodied in critical articles or reviews.

Legal & Disclaimer

The information contained in this ebook is not designed to replace or take the place of any form of medicine or professional medical advice. The information in this ebook has been provided for educational & entertainment purposes only.

The information contained in this book has been compiled from sources deemed reliable, and it is accurate to the best of the Author's knowledge; however, the Author cannot guarantee its accuracy and validity and cannot be held liable for any errors or omissions. Changes are periodically made to this book. You must consult your doctor or get professional medical advice before using any of the suggested remedies, techniques, or information in this book.

Upon using the information contained in this book, you agree to hold harmless the Author from and against any damages, costs, and expenses, including any legal fees potentially resulting from the application of any of the information provided by this guide. This disclaimer applies to any damages or injury caused by the use and application, whether directly or indirectly, of any advice or information presented, whether for breach of contract, tort, negligence, personal injury, criminal intent, or under any other cause of action.

You agree to accept all risks of using the information presented inside this book. You need to consult a professional medical practitioner in order to ensure you are both able and healthy enough to participate in this program.

Table Of Contents

Introduction 1

Chapter 1: Understanding Effective Cold-Calling 3

Chapter 2: How To Keep Up With Industry Changes 11

Chapter 3: "Characteristics Of Great Cold-Callers" 16

Chapter 4: Highly Valuable Strategies And Tips To Be Successful 21

Chapter 5: Writing Your Own Scripts 30

Chapter 6: Prospect With Dignity 33

Chapter 7: Vital Marketing Concepts 57

Chapter 8: Surviving A Market That Is Hard Market 91

Chapter 9: Network Marketing And The End Of Stealth Prospecting 123

Chapter 10: Mid-Size Manufacturing Firms Need More Effective Marketing 143

Conclusion 182

Introduction

You're probably new to the job and you've just completed your debut in sales.Your job is now contingent on your skills in the field of cold-calling. You might be worried about the future of your financial performance and just so.Cold calling is by far the most competitive field in the business-to-business or business-to-consumer models However, that's not always negative. A lot of people think of cold-calling as an "numbers game" but the reality could not be further as this.

The reality is that cold-calling can be an experience of trial-by-fire, the test that makes the top sales managers as they speak.While many salespeople who cold-call do not meet their target but those who are able to stand out from the crowd end up becoming incredibly efficient powerful, influential, and successful players in the game of sales. This is the way you should approach it , too, should you want to perform very well in the game.

Stop worrying about your future and change your outlook to reflect a positive outlook.Great salespeople don't stare at the competitive market and say "Oh I'm so sorry.

There's so many people that are fighting myself," but rather they look at the situation with a smile at the thought "Awesome! The huge number of competitors will reduce the competition and create less competition on my part!" If you can see the distinction between the two strategies similar to what happens when gladiators who are forced to be dragged screaming and kicking into a arena, or walking into with their heads up and weapons readyyou're on the way to becoming a memorable salesperson.

This book will explain the fundamentals of successful cold-calling, the challenges faced by this aspect of business, and how you can avoid these; as well as the many techniques, tips and methods you should use to stay ahead and make yourself a god in the crowd of salespeople. Let's get started!

Chapter 1: Understanding Effective Cold-Calling

Like we said that cold-calling is the most competitive element of sales in any field. Before we go on to the details of this industry, we'll ensure that you're aware of this particular version of Hunger Games in which you've fallen head-first. Am I frightening you? Good. This will make your joy at the conclusion of the book more evident.

Cold-calling is the process is a art form by itself, of contacting an uninitiated person without not having any idea what you're about or the country you're from. In essence, they don't have any reason to believe in your business, and the majority of them aren't even interested in the product or service you're selling. Even if your sales team has already identified their target market and has conducted some sort of demographic targeting and supplied you with numbers to match, this isn't much to increase your chance of getting a positive response.

In contrast to warm-calling, in which the customer at opposite end has had a conversation with you whether directly or indirectly and is waiting for your call, cold-callers must overcome a variety of obstacles, like time constraints on the other hand and a distrustful attitude towards phone-based sales, or just consumers who aren't interested.

While many tried to decipher the basic principles from the practices of masters of cold-calling in the past, no effort to develop a foolproof method for this specific type of call has ever been able to work. This implies that there's more to cold-calling that simple phrases, words, speech patterns and even scripts. The reaction towards each cold-caller is likely to be more chemical, similar to when voters pick their presidential candidates on the basis of more than the tone of their political opinions.

In contrast to realtors, car salesmen and other salespeople that deal with clients face-to-face cold-callers carry out the entire range of their responsibilities via phone calls, which means they can throw things like looks or gender, clothing sensitivities, personality, mannerisms and physical appeals out of the picture. The main factors that appear to be absent--the acuity of what separates a successful cold-caller from someone who's out of work are energy confidence, confidence, lilt, the tone of voice in addition to the capability to comprehend situations and create responses on the spot based upon the tone and lilt of the client's voice. But, unless you commit to learning how to master social communication abilities, understanding the smallest subtleties of a conversation may be beyond your ability.

Recent studies have revealed the fact that only 35% or less of cold callers achieve their monthly sales goals without any consistency The majority of cold-callers are able to only achieve around 40 percent of expected sales goals, if they even manage to reach them. This should give you a an picture of the extent of the problem you're in.

But, you'll only feel this is threatening if believe you'll be unsuccessful rather than succeed, essentially stating that you don't have confidence. If you want to be a winner in this area and the rewards of being successful are immense--not just for your current position, but also in terms of your chances of rapid advancement and progression within the ranks of your company, you need to put your feet up and let go of your doubts, and begin to believe in yourself with greater confidence. Confidence is the key word in the game, and it's easily made up until the cows are home.

Furthermore, even though cold-calling has numerous drawbacks, it provides two significant advantages to any person in the field: it has no requirement for a degree or certifications, nor is it required to enhance your skill sets to be a better cold-caller and gives the highest rate of growth for those who succeed in sales. This makes it ideal for a time where everybody and their grandmother are interacting through Facebook and where young people are becoming disenchanted by traditional college programs. A lot of people are now looking for professions that reward the ability to make decisions on your own, instincts and skills that can be improved through experience, and the rewards of thriving in competitive and crowded environments, just like entrepreneurs, stock brokers, or venture capitalists. Instead of not letting this profession intimidate you, take an extra step, place yourself in the mindset that of an actor in the method and start to conquer your sales targets.

Before we move to the next step, it is imperative to look at one of the most important aspects of cold-calling. Many people believe that because you've been provided with lists of 50 to 70 potential customers at once (as an instance) and your monthly quota for sales is to sell around 1,000 units of your product -- it's the game of numbers, and you get some wins and you lose some. Beware of this view--it's the perspective of those who lose in the game of sales.

This kind of understanding will eventually hurt you in the main reason that you don't lose a few clients and you also lose a hell of lots. The best salespeople are proud of their work and treat each client as a jewel in their belt. They do not want to engage with any potential customer with a sloppy approach, primarily because they see each call as a test through which they develop their capabilities. For those who rose from the field, every conversation isn't about just one person from three hundred in the list it's about whether or not they are capable of closing any type of client that might come across their paths.

Additionally, even though it might be an "numbers game" for many, novice cold-callers are often unable to appreciate the enormous limitations placed on them by each list offered. For instance, if you stick to the statistics, and you follow the rules, then about 65% of those working on sales floors will not be able to reach even 50% of their target quota every month. What occurs when you're given roughly 2 000 numbers every month, and only have to sell thousands of products (as as an illustration)? This is due to the fact that you require each of your calls to result in a sale, if you let things run their normal path, the actual figure could be more like one out of twelve. Therefore, particularly since your marketing departments are sure to have provided lists of feasible demographically-targeted people for your product, the pressure on you to convert and close is far higher than normal. Although it could have been a numbers-based game if you had an unlimited number of numbers, your list of customers to call is very limited. Every caller who you or a coworker does not convert to a buyer in the first attempt is less likely to buy your product, even if a different person contacts them later. Thus, each call that your colleagues make doesn't only cut off that customer (for an amount of time) to them, but it also affects you and the reverse is true.

The most significant issue of using the "numbers game" method is that it teaches the mentality of rationalizing the failures and weaknesses which hinders you from progressing. Sales generally (cold-calling including cold-calling) does not aim at satisfying an need that the clients already recognized they have, but one they'd never thought of. This isn't about selling Ice to an Saharan however, but for an Alaskan Inuit. So, excuses like "they were not in the market" or "they weren't in the mood or the need to purchase this product" can only be used as excuses, not as facts. If experienced and successful salespeople are able convert those customers to consumers that you could too, and every other reason is an excuse to cover up your lack of ability to do the same.

I can see the familiar look of disgust on your face. The one that originates from the depths of our souls when we are confronted by the realities of sales. However, don't worry. We'll leave your moral dilemmas for you in upcoming chapters.

Chapter 2: How To Keep Up With Industry Changes

And I can tell this for certain 7 out of eight of you who read this chapter would have developed feelings of disgust following the final paragraphs of the chapter before--and I completely appreciate your viewpoint. It's not just you as it's actually the person who is looking down, not the salesperson. This is the most significant issue in the sales industry in the past few years: they've totally and totally ruined it for everyone else.

For centuries, dealing with salespeople who are slick and sweet has resulted in consumers having an apparent aversion to the business of selling and most are completely unwilling to give salespeople the chance to talk with them or even to listen to 15-second elevator pitches. If you think about it, before becoming an salesperson How many cold calls were you subjected to from those who were trying to convince you of something or attempting to convince you to sign up for credit cards or even an upgrade plan for your cell phone? What number of calls did you have to deal with and how many actually held your attention for the entire duration in their selling pitch?

This is the time to refute the assertion I made previously. Although the reality in sales lies that persistent silver-tongued, tenacious people prevail over other people, it does not mean you have to be a pushy, rude or adamantly intent on chanting "buy buy, buy and buy" via the headset to your client as long as you can be able to do it. The rising popularity of the field of sales has brought about a dramatic change that is reflected in the vast books that teach you how to be more effective cold-callers with no negative traits that turn customers off with "Hello !"--and this book is designed to provide practical assistance.

The effectiveness of these changes can be evident in the success of the new generation of sales professionals who have reached their top heights, yet have not lost the attention of their individual customers with every contact they've placed. Instead of creating demands with false advertisements or overblown claims The new approach to cold-calling has been laid on the foundations of three essential principles: the connection between the consumer and caller and the honesty of the sales-caller and the genuine care of the salesperson for their product's possible use to consumers.

If you are employed by a mid-to-large business, it is likely that your marketing or sales department has already done some sort of demographic targeting following the identification of the majority of customers who might be interested in your product. Once they've done that they'd given you the names of those who are more likely of purchasing your product and bringing you greater chances of success than if you picked random numbers from directories of telephone numbers. Thus, the possibility that you sell ice products to Inuit in the sense of will be greatly diminished since you'll mainly dealing with those in the same client base that buys your product regardless. In this case, half the work is done for you , all you have to accomplish is to close the sale. I won't be boring you with tales of how difficult cold-calling used be with no demographic targeting when I was in the "good good old times" Keep in mind that these periods in the past had lower sales figures for top performers as you do in the present.

Take a moment to listen, because the workplace environment hasn't significantly changed from this view. Cold-callers remain in cubicles or small offices, handed scripts they are expected to view as holy scripture, and handed virtual lists of potential customers are expected to convert into customers to meet their sales targets. The basic pay is still poor, and individuals are expected to cover the difference between their needs and real incomes by earning commissions from sales in a variety of organizations. However, these types of environments transform you into a member of the crowd, but not the secret gem inside it. But, and this is the one that can save your bacon: companies do not care about how you make deals as long as you're able to get customers. This is a well-known sales behavior that you'll be able to exploit within businesses so that you don't need to be a victim of customers or just another desk jockey who is barely making ends meet , and falling short of your sales targets every month.

Like I mentioned earlier, one of the largest changes in the mentality of cold-calling gurus has been the inclusion of the abovementioned pillars--relationship, integrity, and concern. The most obvious result of this paradigm shift is that scripts although still vital in the business, aren't believed to be infallible and sacrosanct. While they can to keep you on track by providing speaking details, they're cookie cutter design immediately turns off the majority of consumers.

The first thing the best cold-callers do is either modify any script they've received from their corporate partners to make it more appropriate to their own individual personalities and eloquence or, they utilize the lessons learned from each call to create their own scripts in the first few days of starting their new position. This gives them the benefit of avoiding the ruts that trap salespeople in monotonous, zombie-like messages that result from repeated repeating the exact same message over and over, and helps them maintain lively, engaging conversations with their clients and also give them with the ability and ability to steer conversations in a way that will yield sales that are confirmed by responding to feedback that they receive through the subtle tones of their customers' voices.

Chapter 3: "Characteristics Of Great Cold-Callers"

No matter if you're a cold-caller warm-caller traits that make you successful in this area will be the exact same. Recognizing and improving these characteristics will, in the near future, guarantee your credibility as a reputable salesperson.

The best cold-callers are those with improved social skills and the capacity to create a clear, engaging conversation about any topic. The ability to communicate effectively doesn't have to be developed by being a through a random encyclopedia however, it is developed through the development of different opinions and the capacity to defend these opinions when confronted. In essence, even if the information you're saying isn't backed by any facts, keep the confidence and a calm manner when giving your opinion that will cause the person who is speaking to you doubt their understanding and grasp of the issue, instead of revealing your lack or any other way. However, if you discover that you're not equipped in a particular area of your life, try your best to inform yourself about the issue, but never let your confidence or calm be lost in the eyes of someone other.

The best cold-callers are masters at vocal subtleties. That means you must be able, with the tiny amount of information you receive from the other side of the phone call--the attitude of the customer who is just a simple "Hello". Therefore, you must be able to alter your pitch each time based on the significance of the information interpreted by your gut. If, for instance, the customer is extremely angry skilled cold-callers do not rely with the "bubbly smiley voice" because it angers these customers instead of helping to help them calm down. If you're feeling like they are losing interest due to attempts to engage them from their side or if they're displaying audible signs of boredom, you must be able to shift tracks and include fascinating "hooks" or information that could be used as a reference to the product you're selling, or that will help customers who are unsure to make better decisions for you.

Although the best cold-callers are as focused on bottom line and sales as other sales reps, if not much more, they realize that presenting the product the same way for every client isn't effective. Therefore, their methods must be tailored to the person they're communicating. Even though poor salespeople might be able to protest their methods of interaction, the strategies that result in a purchase are different dramatically between young and old people, or even between men as well as women in some cases.

It is also important not to generalize across populations. Try to analyse every bit of information you collect from every word spoken by a client to improve your strategy. Start with something as simple as how they introduce themselves or respond to your phone when they receive your phone. To comprehend these differences you must develop your social skills so that you can recognize the motivations that drive the actions of various people. Thus, a common trait of the most successful cold-callers is they're socially inclined and are constantly seeking out social interactions instead of avoiding them.

If you've not been an extremely social person in the past, don't fret this is the perfect opportunity to begin as could be any. If you invest as much time in enhancing your social skills as you do worrying regarding your new position, you'll begin knowing the motives behind various types of people within a matter of minutes. And when you've done that you'll see a dramatic increase in your sales skills.

The best cold-callers are also aware of the importance of following up. Sometime, customers are too busy to be paying the attention of sales messages, and in these instances, abruptly cut off and abandon the call before you've had the opportunity to explain to them the features of your service. When this happens, good cold-callers know how to be respectful of their customers by not bombarding them with frequent calls. Instead of marking off these clients as unsuccessful prospects, they record the clients as failed and attempt to contact them the day or next day following, when they feel is appropriate. The cooling-off period permits clients to put the contact to the back of their mind, and lessens the likelihood of receiving being met with a hostile response in the next attempt. Only after you've had the chance to talk about your product and the customer has clearly rejected any interest, do you mark such clients as a failed prospect.

In addition, good cold-callers are able to devise strategies to address different sections of the population efficiently. This involves factors like the most effective timing to contact for each as well as the most common opening response or types of interactions you must follow for each one along with closing remarks that will likely trigger buttons in the mind of the customer and push them to make final the deal in your favor. Again, this particular ability is mostly determined through experience and diverse social interactions--although we will be discussing some of these tips in the subsequent chapter.

Chapter 4: Highly Valuable Strategies And Tips To Be Successful

1. Know Your Sales Materials in depth

The best orators study their speeches in complete detail before they attempt to deliver their speeches on stage, without prompts or cards. They are often perceived as being the most authentic innovative, engaging, convincing, and captivating during their interaction with the audiences. This is because when you understand your content completely, it frees your mind to express enthusiasm or charm into what you call your "sales pitch" in the end, and every speech that is written with a purpose in mind is one type or another of selling pitch.

Thus, you should be familiar with all the information that is available about the product you're selling, including specifications, manufacturing specifications that are necessary to know, recent big sales to well-known corporations or individuals, market satisfaction data, unique ways to use the product that were praised by previous customers, and any sales guides, documents or brochures that may have been given from your company. If you think there are any significant issues with the materials that you have received, or any other information you believe you must know, as it may be useful to customers you can ask your bosses. Any person who understands the ins and outs of selling will be impressed by your determination to know more and beyond the basics that many of your colleagues are unable to fully read at first.

If you're no longer switching between different the pages of your manual trying to respond to customers asking questions, or find information that clients might appreciate, you'll be able spend your entire time to understanding the personality of the person you're talking to and determine the best method of communication that will appeal for them most. This will instantly set you apart from the crowds of sales floor zombies cold-callers that fail to solicit purchases from customers every day. They even dissuade customers who could be a perfect fit for any salesperson who has mediocre abilities.

2. Continue to tweak your Method based on the Demographic

Although this could be an exaggeration, some opening strategies work best for particular demographics.

For instance, if you're talking to a customer who is in their teens Don't try to bombard the client with a lot of technical details. For the majority clients, the image of the product as raising their social standing and status , while also being an excellent bargain at the price is more effective than any details of the product's technical features all. It is possible to alter this as there's a substantial subset of teenagers who are educated and responsible consumers and require additional information before they make a decision. If the customer you're speaking to falls into the latter category the client will be interested in any additional information that is of their interest and you don't have to consider which sub-set of teens that you're talking to. However, in this group, the most appropriate time to reach them is typically in the afternoon the time that any classes they could be taking have concluded and it's not too late to disrupt any late-night social activities they might have planned for themselves.

Another instance is that for middle-aged and working women when it is the most appropriate time to call is early in the morning, or in the late afternoons or early evenings before the time to head back home. This is due to the fact that these are the times that they're either going to work, and then stuck in traffic, or finishing up work and heading to home. It is not necessary to call them back since they are busy with conferences or meetings. In addition, for those with these types of people - particularly those who are likely to take the phone by calling them by calling them professionally rather than just a monotone "Hi" the most effective strategy is to talk about the purpose of your product and the recent sales and bargains deals with well-known or large organizations that might have been a part of your product. They may also be unable to handle exuberant sales staff, consequently, it's recommended to keep a calm and friendly, while maintaining a professional in your tone.

For women and men who prefer to work at home or who are homemakers and prefer to work from home, it is best to contact them just before or after lunchtime, though it could be different for each client. This is due to the human tendency of slowing down prior to lunch, or the post-lunch time that is enjoyed by many, but there is a difference starkly in a subset.

Although they may appear as generalizations, they could be slightly from your personal experience humans operate according to the law of massive numbers. It is on you to identify the most effective sales strategy and the best timing to use that will be most effective for the intended audience for your item. Although humans are very individual in various ways, these strategies are generally applied in a general way because they are largely dependent on the time of day and the mental strategies that people create within their own organizations and companies, who prefer methods of uniformity that facilitate better functioning. It is also possible to use your personal experiences to in the development of these strategies. For instance, if, for example, you're a young person in your early 20s working for a major corporation with fixed lunch hours and lunch hours, when would be the ideal time to call you, and manage to gain a bit of your attention and time? Don't be averse to being part of the defined demographic whether you're or been member of this group in the past. Your personal experiences as a teenager for instance, could be a valuable source of information to come up with strategies by asking yourself about strategies of sales and conversation that have helped you through your teens.

This type of understanding of demographics and the use of different strategies for each one is a cherished business concept that is widely admired by the top salespeople. It also forms an integral part of modern-day marketing campaign planning.

3. Use Energy to Your Benefit

The most significant obstacle for most cold-callers is their acceptance of their own apathy and resignation towards their job. Imagine if you had the chance to speak to salespeople who appear to be completely uninterested in their product? Do you prefer to meet with people who seem to truly believe in their product's potential to enhance your life and seem very eager to share their product with you?

Thus be sure to bring enthusiasm and energy for each call you make. It's not that you must behave as if your overdosing on Prozac but you should not sound exhausted angry, irritable, or simply trying to complete things that are bothersome to you.

The most effective way to accomplish this is to not sit on your feet while making your phone call. Even even if you're in an office cubicle, get up and move around when you make every phone call. It's true, this is effective. The enthusiasm you're putting into it will always result in an enjoyable conversation for your customer, and will let your brain perform better when it tries to perfect your technique on each call. Even if it seems odd and perhaps a little odd to colleagues but your bosses will not care when it turns into sales.

In such instances it is also possible to use the power pose, such as standing in Superman fashion with your chest up with your hands on your hips, with your legs are just a bit more than your shoulders. There are other similar methods to increase your confidence when making phone calls. Power poses are well-known and admired techniques that can boost confidence, enhance creative interactions, and boost your ability to speak with confidence in public speaking. This will aid to connect with your customers.

4. Don't provide clients with convenient ways to leave

This is among the most common mistakes that new salespeople make. When speaking to customers make sure you don't say things like "would would you prefer to learn about our latest product?" or "can I take a minute to spare your time?" or even "would you be interested in this or that product we offer?" While this may be a bit insensitive, it's actually the easiest to turn down and is the most efficient method for someone to walk off the line when they're in a hurry or simply don't want to bother. Your response isn't always indicative of their opinions about the product being discussed.

Do not ask a question that would allow the customer to respond with "No Thank you" and close the conversation. Once they've picked up the phone the only question you need to ask is whether the same type of product like your vacuum cleaner, has been causing them issues recently since it's not functioning like it did before and then whether they'd like to purchase one right now or if you need to schedule a phone call for the next few days from now to ensure they have enough time. In this moment you've already completed your sales pitch in the sense of in the event that they don't want to buy, they'll simply let you know at this point and then end the conversation. This way you'll have time to give your best to be heard without getting the phone slammed into your face after just five seconds of the conversation.

Chapter 5: Writing Your Own Scripts

The use of scripts, even though they're shunned by some of the greatest to encourage spontaneous interactions, they still play a significant element, particularly for novices to the world of cold-calling. Although you'll likely be given a sales script when you work in a large-sized company however, the standard cookie-cutter sales message is unproductive when cold-calling and can only be effective in warm-calling.

So, when you've begun working, you must write your own script right from the very beginning. Although it's possible to be disapproved of by bosses and looked at by coworkers I can assure you that your creativity in this particular project will result in substantial returns, both in terms of greater closure rates and greater appreciation from superiors.

To develop your personal script, you'll need the following components: a diagram of opening lines based on the recognition of demographics from their own introductions once customers take their calls and a second step that provides a quick overview of the product's purpose and uses and the sales strategy you've identified to be effective for that particular audience (as we've covered earlier in this chapter) and any other quick details and interesting details about recent awards or big sales to notable companies or individuals (as as it doesn't affect any privacy policies implemented by your company) in the final step, which concludes with discount or bargain offers for customers to consider who have confirmed an the order as soon as they received it.

You can create various scripts to suit various demographics or compile your scripts based on experience into one diagram that you then use to guide your way through conversations. If you're a big fan of The Big Bang Theory, the result will be similar to Sheldon's diagram for making friends for example. I personally like this method since it lets me modify my method in any situation as well as avoiding the time looking through a stack of papers in search of the perfect script. Be sure to keep a small amount of sales-related material in your possession and then condense any information from them that you consider valuable to the script itself instead of needing to search through a variety of sources in search of one piece of information.

Chapter 6: Prospect With Dignity

Are you in your bed, contemplating your monthly bills at late at night? Do you not even meet your monthly volume goal?

Salespeople who are always looking for a less stressful experience than the typical salesperson. We ensure that there is the steady flow of business. Sales reps are aware that they have to look at the door, but they must make every effort to keep it from happening.

Indoor members aren't the only ones to are avoiding potential customers. I know of an outside dealer who's method is to head to the dining area that has a magazine in the lobby, and to erase all of the cards (those that are placed on them on their company cards) and bring them back to the office to serve as an evidence for sales phone calls. There's also the outside representative who is able to sleep three days a week, and her boss thinks she's in the field with customers.

Why is prospecting not taking place? If I ask the same question to my students and the responses I get are : I dislike being dismissed, and I don't have any idea what else to try. I'm feeling like I'm trying to find a company. After hearing the responses I'm able to conclude that the most important conclusion is that leasing professionals don't enjoy prospecting since it's just not running smoothly.

This is why we face two challenges that are aimed at encouraging us to think in the future.

Make sure you are able to look at things in the right way to have fun.

Let's look at the first. What can you do to think about the future?

Repair of the engine visually Julia Mancuso won the silver medal at the 2010 Winter Olympics in Whistler, British Columbia, for women's downhill skiing. In this competition she was not scheduled to win the medal. Swedish and Austrian athletes are seeded higher.

In 10th place, a few skiers were ahead of the best Mancuso ripped a stunning race from beginning to end. Mancuso had been noticed near the start and had her eyes shut and arms mimicking her run through her hair. "I used a lot of imagination and then became violent," stated Mancuso.

If Mancuso had been negative and was anxious, uncertain insecure, or unprepared she may not have been awarded an award. It's the same with prospecting. Think positively and pick up the phone and then wait for a phone call, and anticipate that a relationship will begin and you'll succeed more.

This process is referred to as an engine visual rehearsal. Studies have proven that the same neurons are firing inside your brain when you're performing an activity through your mind, as if you were actually doing the task. This happens to Olympic athletes, NASA astronauts, and highly successful salespeople. Imagine how you can reach your objectives. Think about how you can achieve your goals. be positive about yourself!

You can take a moment to settle down and then imagine how you feel when you hit your income goals. Imagine contacting prospects and landing your ideal client successfully. When you contact vendors, you're hesitant to be confident in yourself. What would you think of if you were totally confident? What would you hear, see? How will you move and talk? Do you seem moving or slow with your movements? Do you feel excited or bored? Make it appear as if you trust yourself and you will see it take place.

What's the most effective method to approach your look now that you're inspired?

Submissions The best method to start is to reach out to people you are familiar with. Call customers you already have, figure out the needs of them, and ask for references. Be persistent in demanding references! If you've got more reference sources, fewer calls you have to make. Your customers should ask "Who is someone you've met that would benefit from working with an excellent leasing firm?" The question should be addressed by asking "Do you have any connections?" If you ask "what you've heard about," they are talking about their connections and could gain a lead.

LinkedIn is a way to create references. Make a list of your most popular ten LinkedIn accounts you wish to join. Check the business you've chosen to join for contacts and request an email introduction. This is an excellent way to concentrate your efforts. Keep in mind that the goal is to seek out respectability. This means that you should focus on your ideas and facts. Provide suggestions to provide solutions for your customers ' issues.

The best Days & Nights The Best Days and Nights. James Oldroyd from Kellogg School of Management recently completed a study. Oldroyd looked over one million calls to cold numbers from databases online that were made by thousands of marketing professionals from 50 companies. He then utilized statistical metrics to identify patterns of failure and success.

Oldroyd says his belief that Thursday's the most effective day to reach out to leads to get qualified. It's about 20 percent more effective than Friday, which is the most difficult day. Each day's in between.

The ideal time to be looking forward to is in the early dawn (8-9 AM)) and in the late in the afternoon (4-5 5 pm).

The research conducted by Oldroyd discovered that the most unfavorable timing to make a call was after lunch. Calls made on a Saturday morning can be 164% more likely than calling between 1 and 2 at night.

The researcher also discovered that you have only 24 hours to validate the leads generated through your website and then move it into your pipelines within the financial services sector. The pressure will be gone after 24 hours.

If we are able to draw conclusions from his findings, we'll hold Friday sales meetings internally at 11:30 am.

Plan prospecting sessions for Thursdays in the morning or late afternoon. Avoidance on Fridays, and especially in the afternoons on Fridays.

Conduct a cold-call in accordance with the degree to which "hot" leads are. If your site is streaming constantly, always make the first calls. Contact those that have been harvested the most recently first to get leads for other leads in your web search.

You may contact a hot lead and get a great recommendation but if you simply chat with the prospect you will forget when you need to pay. It is important to be consistently consistent no matter where you are. Utilize forums, email and direct mail to help improve your work on mobile.

Make sure you are focusing on landing opportunities for big landlords and vendors.

Visualize yourself succeeding and take action in a variety of channels. If you do this every night, you'll rest comfortably.

Focus on landing possibilities for large rental and vendor. Imagine yourself being successful and acting in a variety of channels. If you are like this every night, you'll rest comfortably.

Prospects to talk to You

Do you really have time to consider what makes you think of yourself as a potential or customer? Should you be concerned over the value of your call? Calls to new prospects as well as existing customers remain one of the most vital marketing and business methods you can employ every day. With all the digital tools for communication and marketing Many companies require people to find and establish actual relationships with their customers. The best salespeople ensure that prospecting is an integral part of their routine.

Like most things it is a procedure for entrepreneurs, and as such you'll need to go through it 500-1000 times in a year, or around the same amount of times!

But, a lot of people aren't looking at their screens and some find it to be a burden.

According to me, a large portion of the debate over the 'do not call' debate focuses on the credibility of the calls made. A large portion of the people spoken of aren't achieving their goals in prospecting. They usually make calls and force their desires on other people regardless of another individual's desires or needs. The majority of the time, these calls aren't about you.

Rule 1 of Prospect: You have to have a keen interest in very first possibility of connecting with someone else, and make them interested in your company and what you can offer them.

As a contrast, if they asked you (very briefly) about who they were, they showed respect for your commitments to time when they asked whether you would like to talk to them right now or later and then swiftly and courteously explained the reason they wanted you to connect (all of them were mentioned in your perspective and to your own benefit) If you were asked, take a minute to find out the person you thought they were.

From the perspective of the prospective client or customer from the perspective of the prospect or client, there should be an incentive to contact you. Something that will enhance your life in some way. It is likely that you would like to partner with them as they might be in your ideal market or could be an important customer that you can be a part of the team to earn money, build a image, etc.

Consider the reason someone who is a prospect or customer is interested in speaking with you. Research and think about the reason they'd like to make the effort to speak with you. Imagine yourself in their shoes or in other words.

You might be their hero however, if they don't recognize that they must be saved, and you're not certain whether they'd prefer not to be saved and you're not sure if they want to be saved, you're in danger.

Contact will bring value to your customer starting with the initial phone call until thanking them after the first meeting , and any subsequent ones. There has to be a legitimate motive behind every touch.

In most cases, the phone call is often the initial contact point for potential customers. Two essential elements must be prepared to be prepared for the prospecting call: 1. A Call

Goal- Your call goal is the goal you want to reach.

Why would you like to join this person/divisionor business on behalf of yourself? What are you hoping benefit from the relationship? I.e., i.e. You've heard of an upcoming project under the program and you want to reach out to the stakeholder that is the main decision-maker to find out whether you have a an opportunity to take the project into consideration. Or , you'd like to talk to an influencer who could introduce you to the primary decision maker, etc. 2. The VBR (Valid Business Reason)- It should be meaningful and forward-looking. It must provide a reason of why the prospect should desire to learn more about the person. It should be valuable and relevant for the coming years and be able to react to what's in it from the viewpoint of your potential customers.

Most of the time, VBRs are not static but are rather constantly changing and evolving. It is essential to update it to reflect the present business environment as well as market trends. VBR requires salespersons to get their minds off of their own products and examine the market and the larger world in which they work. There's no shortage of VBAC.

Here are a few categories which can enable you to build VBR's: Competitor Reality Timing & seasonal fit class Performance New place / Growth Broaden the business focus Comparison -- Personal intro Site visitor match activities/opportunities New concept/idea Hear anyone who complains of these irritating callings and does not use VBR's.

Prospecting Rule #2: To make success with VBRs make sure you take your mind away from your products and look at your potential customers.

Examine your client or prospective clients and observe what's on your mind , or what's your desire You won't be losing VBR's. The position of VBR in your team is a fantastic opportunity to develop concepts and abilities to make their application successful. This will significantly increase the efficiency in your prospecting via mobile.

A good example of the most successful VBR call can be described like this: "Hallo XXX: This is an Sue phone call coming from Company X;

have you an opportunity to speak?" Say, "yes.". I appreciate your call! We're specialized in helping businesses similar to yours boost their profits by as much as 20% by utilizing the management of our stock management systems.

If they do not say no you can't, they'll tell you... "I know you're busy right now and my phone call is to let know that we specialize in helping businesses like yours to improve the annual profits of their business by 20 percent or more through our inventory management solutions.

Make sure you are in a good place. Before you talk to your prospect or client make sure you provide them with a reason to speak to you.

Prospecting For Clients in Commercial Real Estate

For commercial property it is crucial to be aware of the right people, and a lot of them, and then approach them. They include homeowners tenants, homeowners as well as real estate investors, buyers and sellers. Most successful real estate brokers and agents will reach out to hundreds of these people and would be in contact with them on a regular basis. We reach out to each individual at least every 90 days within their database, and sometimes frequently to build "the bridge of trust and importance." To accomplish this, you must be extremely disciplined with recording and eating and take personal responsibility for your prospecting task.

In essence the commercial and investment real estate market is focused on people who have real estate problems and issues. Your company should provide the solution they're seeking, and your solution must be superior to your brokers and competitors. What are your thoughts taking forward? Don't lie and say you're familiar with the industry. You've concluded the deal. You're the top person in the room with the most effective team. You're the top communication expert.

For the past 100 years you've been on the market!

The majority of these substances are 'thrown' onto a prospective buyer by normal brokers in nearly every presentation of lease or sale of assets. Make your presentation more effective by presenting real proof, strategy and details. Be confident about your thoughts and beliefs, and also the things you can do and how you are able to do. Look it up! Let it be known! Participate in your own solution to ensure that no other business can fill the need.'

Don't lure your customers with tenting, low-level options like discounted fees or free publicity, since these will be ineffective for good clients. The most loyal customers understand that promoting property effectively and seeking commercial property solutions will cost money and is an extensive strategy. Request your prospective customers' interest to participate in the property solution you had in mind.

We are today blessed with tools that are in line with our current opportunities (databases and electronic mail). It is the personal touch that is more crucial than any other aspect to grow your company , and will remain as such. Personal branding is a crucial element of generating market share for your business and establishing a long-term opportunity. Your customers must know your personal knowledge will provide them with confidence that they will be able to quickly and efficiently solve their property issues. Build your brand each day with a phone appointment and lift without failure. Business cards and lots of them are a great method of tracking your business following each meeting. Forget about the bright brochures and focus on your marketing.

What do you need to know about the first meeting and for the people you'd like to establish an alliance? It's simple: take care of your concerns and issues. They can impede or limit your prospecting time each day. No matter what the market is doing or what the economic situation is the people who are looking the opportunity to rent or buy commercial properties are available. You only need to locate these people and have something to aid you in your listing or toolbox.' You'll get a lot of comments such as "no thank you now" when you phone and talk to a lot of individuals in the field. It is essential to maintain contact with these individuals in case they might need your help. Commercial immobilization is unique and typically the ability of professional agents to successfully close an acquisition or lease is essential. You're highly sought-after but maybe not right now but in the near future.

Lift your skills in communication. It is beneficial when you begin your career to employ and practice script outline outlines particularly for and on phone calls when you are cold. In essence, these scripts should be guidelines, not something to take literally.' Any calls you make should be natural and free of formality of the script. You can make a lot of calls each day, and you can be sure that a lot of people will not be interested. It's the continuous calling process that gives you the chance that you're looking for. In the average, you receive around five rewards or agreements to contact decision-makers when you make 100 phone calls. In time this process creates the"chance tower.' This requires determination to keep the process running and advancing. The best people I've encountered and learned from in the field are able to make about 250 calls per week. Amazing numbers, yes however, they're crucial for success.

In the end, you need an ongoing communication system that collects and stores information daily and requires a control device. If you have a lot of people to talk to and the more you talk to, the better contact recorder or database is required. It's great to utilize Microsoft Outlook in the early stages of your prospecting because it's accessible to the majority of people who use their computers. As more contacts you create the more precise CRM system must be.

Be sure to be sure to ask the right questions. The commercial immobilization business and their customers are typically experienced and can easily spot someone who doesn't know anything about what they are saying or doing. The information you provide to the discussion is vital to the discussion from the very beginning. The goal is to be confident and relevant to the person listening. Commercial property is special unlike residential properties. Be aware of your abilities and increase your awareness and confidence in crucial things like pricing, sales techniques and trends for buyers leases, rents the market, types of buildings and methods for marketing. You should be an expert in walking commercial immobilization information.

The excitement you experience from bringing people you meet with advantages should not be undervalued. These benefits could include access to buyers, sellers owners, tenants developers, investors, databases or market segments. Specific methods of advertising or the nationwide network of offices for property marketing could also prove beneficial. Differentiate yourself from other companies in terms of advantages and be able to convey this to potential customers.

To be successful perseverance, patience, and consistency in your personal prospecting process are vital. It means that you should be prospecting each day. This doesn't mean you should only prospect once per week or whenever you have spare time. It's more important to make a plan to market than listing an estate. Prospecting is at highest point of your funnel's income. Make sure you feed the "funnel" daily and you'll be able to have great success in each market.

It is possible to believe that these important aspects are easily understood when you are evaluating and influencing your commercial immobilization work, but many of the people in the industry aren't always doing so. It is evident that the majority of people working in the industry have a poor understanding of their business and opportunity cycles. The longer you commit to putting these skills into practice more time it takes you to develop your market share and reap rewards. It's as simple as that.

Prospecting is the lifeblood of any salesperson's business

Prospecting is the heartbeat of any salesperson's business, but it is it is also one of the most challenging and challenging tasks. Your motivation to succeed as well as the definition you have of what success is are the most important factor for you. You're not a very good potential candidate if you don't set clearly defined goals and an underlying motivational force that drives you to reach these goals. It's that simple. I'll suggest two methods to fill up you tank. However, at final point, it's about whether you'd like your pipeline full or not. How much is dependent on your motivation, so let's go.

Your motivation, your personal motivation, and your reasons for success are all yours. The ability you have to effectively sell not just in the realm of prospecting, but also throughout all aspects of business expansion determines the direction you take. The top performers tend to follow because they're committed and are convinced of their work and their value, and are able to promote the process continuously. Some people might be offended by the fact that they believe that their "work" is separate from their personal lives and they don't have children for a second. High-performing people love their work, and they network constantly. Why wouldn't you? What are the reasons? If you enjoy your work, have a knack for doing it, and know that you can aid those who are interested, would you not look for opportunities to grow the base of your customers and provide them something they're looking for? It's a simple question Wouldn't you feel pleased to advise that they meet with you in order to determine if they want to buy your product or service, since you know that the products you offer are beneficial to companies? If it's not right to be able to see this, and then either walk out of sales or make an opportunity, you need to prove who you're like, what believein, and fill you with motivation and a purpose. You can only fake it for a short time and my suggestion is to not consider what you are doing in sales until you've given the wholeheartedly.

Prospecting is typically seen in a linear way" What number of calls did you make? "As you go through sales job descriptions and sales job interview questions It is often illustrated, however the interviewer and the interviewer may not be able to understand the purpose for certain reasons. Prospecting is the way to explain. Why do you wish to investigate and see what's in store for you? What is it that draws you to be looking forward? what's your strategy and how do you plan to keep it going?"

One photo that has stuck with me is an arrow that began in a name file and then the dollar signs were visible on the opposite end of the telephone. The idea behind it is that if you are willing to keep going and keep making your phone calls, you'll eventually be successful. However the goal of prospecting is to promote and network and your business or product whenever possible each day. You need to build your brand within your field by adopting this method.

You'll connect your industry colleagues, business contacts through hyperlinks, friends and relatives in your market of choice.

Join the chamber of commerce networks as well as unions, business organizations or non-profit groups, charities Toastmasters, your area and the culture. Join a club or company and play a significant part in making your profile more prominent. It's a good idea to supplement this strategy with high-quality by providing engaging content, interactive information, and presentations when feasible such as conferences, workshops writing ups, newsletters and write-ups as well as a great online presence. It is also essential to dedicate yourself to personal learning by studying, listening to education CDs, taking part in workshops and continue to pursue continuing training to be able to successfully implement this plan. You have to be an expert within your business-otherwise how will you prove it and what benefits do you offer? The most viable approach is the first one. I'll call it "dollars dialing." If you're using it be sure to keep an eye on dials, calls made , meetings orders, and marketing revenue. Calculate the amount of profit per calls you call. If, for instance, there are 300 phone calls which produce three sales and $30,000 of revenues, every when you use your mobilephone, you will earn $100. You'll be able to make solid calls if you know this measurement. What if you could make 400 calls If you can raise another $10,000? Engage in making several calls per week. Alternate your call times and monitor the day and time you'll succeed. This will help you improve your efficiency. It is important to contact people between 08:00 and 17:00-006:00, as those times are the best method to contact individuals, specifically managers and supervisors. Buddy together, participate in exercises in a group and have some amusement. It creates an atmosphere that is more competitive as well as an overall sense of camaraderie when everyone does. Keep your optimism and carry your passion to work. If your brand isn't positive and optimistic, what do you envision it to look? Managers and supervisors must be part of the solution! If you're scared or feel "below your level," then what kind of message are you conveying to your staff. For instance Set the tone and then take the phone.

Prepare yourself and know what you can tell them when you get an email with an outlook. The goal is to encourage people to engage regularly and in the early hours. Begin with a brief introduction, and a list of smart questions to ask. You should make an objective phone call. Discovery through the phone could be scheduled at a suitable time or on a schedule for a meeting. Always follow the deal with caution. Build and invest in solid database and list. Have a geographically-defined business prospecting strategy , and utilize quantitative elements to support strategic goals. You divide your accounts into medium, high, as well as low-priority accounts. Spend more time on building medium and high priority accounts. Create your own server in-house to record conversations, calls contacts' names, along with follow-up calendars. Your internal archive will grow into your main source of prospecting as time passes. Make it a priorityto be busy and dial. I've seen representatives too of the time let their dedication slip in prospecting. Don't let it occur to you.

Chapter 7: Vital Marketing Concepts

Marketing is now a crucial element of any business. The cost to sell an item is greater, however, the focus of advertising is focused on the buying and selling of producer and consumer behaviors due to a variety of motives (e.g. the monopoly market or the oligopoly market and niche market). Marketing is a process whereby goods and services are sold from producers to consumers. A successful advertisement is "The best product or service that will bring you profit at the right location at the right time , and at the correct cost." The United states Marketing Association defines the institutions, activities and processes that are used to create communication, deliver, and exchange goods that have significance for customers, clients and others. The Marketing Association defines the following definition of formal. The focus of sales is for sellers to transform their products into cash, and to promote the notion that customers' needs are met by the product as well as the whole array of items that are connected to animals. A study by Market and App Data Room found that branding and sales alignment can increase the value of the product by 70 percent at the time of the purchase. This will reduce the pressure by 108% and increase the potential for marketing value by 209 percent. "The advertising and. branding cycle can damage the reputation of a business by just only one word or phrase. A study by the American Marketing Association describes a branding as the name, a term logo, mark or design, or any combination of them, that is designed to differentiate and distinguish between the services or products and the competition of a single retailer or group of retailers.' Brand Equity is the name of the brand's reputation due to its long-lasting recognition and trustworthiness which results in more sales and higher profits than other brands in the marketplace. Internal branding is a crucial element of strategic planning in the creation of brand equity. When launching a brand an authority in marketing or contractor will take four different perspectives to develop an effective brand-consumer perspective (to assess the value of the product or service for a range of customers) A Perspective from the Company (to enhance, either technically or aesthetically, the appearance of the product or service and the third). The brand is what you represent when you make public statements and influence the decision-making of consumers. Thus, the function of branding or managing brands is the process of marketing that includes the analysis and development of the position of the brand in the marketplace, targeted towards the public as well as the safeguarding of a good brand's reputation. A company or an entrepreneur advertises their products or services to prospective buyers via advertisements. Advertising can be defined as "Any kind of pay-per-click communication." Most popular marketing outlets are pressed and digital, as well as, and social media. In essence, marketing is the strategy or method used to convince prospective buyers to purchase the best product or service. Advertising translates marketing strategies into various media. The goal is to convince potential customers in advertisements that they've got the correct product or service. The most pressing issue nowadays is the overwhelming. Cluttering. Cluttering. "The clutter is defined as the volume of messages that the consumer is constantly exposed on a daily basis." The most important task of marketers is managing the overwhelming amount of messages. The most difficult part of managing the clutter is finding the ideal time to speak with customers you want to reach and providing the best feedback regarding your company's situation.

Marketing is different from. Networking The concept of networking is one that involves a system human interaction with other individuals. Networking in the corporate world is always linked to efficient marketing. Corporate networking is a result of the socio-economic experiences of entrepreneurs. It is a circle of corporate networks. It is important to note that Business circles are an element of the larger socio-economic circle that an entrepreneur has. If there isn't a proper collaboration between all the economic actors and shareholders the company will not succeed or grow at all, or even reach its full potential. In order to build an efficient business network, managers and their associates from a broad social and economic circle are crucial. The secret to successful advertising is network, BtoB as well as BtoC.

Effective marketing includes networking, branding, advertising sales and promotions. Networking allows consumers to be targeted at specific areas, while branding allows for creating standards or reforming them, and customer interactions. Advertisements communicate these messages through various product or services, and Marketing encourages consumers to purchase and then the real profits are realized. Marketing is now an essential element of any company. The price of sales for the product is higher but the emphasis of advertisements is on the purchasing and selling of producer and consumer behaviour due to various motives (e.g. Monopoly Competition or the oligopoly market as well as niche markets). Marketing is a process that involves the transfer of goods or services are transferred from the manufacturer to customers. A successful advertising strategy is "The best product or service to profit from it at the right location and at the appropriate time , and at the correct cost." The United states Marketing Association defines the processes, institutions, and processes that are used to create communication, deliver, and exchange products that provide significance for customers, clients and others. The Marketing Association defines the following definition of formal. The focus of sales is to convert sellers' items into cash, in order to promote the notion that customers' needs are met by the product, and also the variety of other things that go with animals. A study conducted by Market and App Data Room found that branding and sales aligning will boost the revenue of the product by 70 percent at the time of the purchase. This will reduce the pressure by 108% and increase the value of marketing of 209 percent. "The advertising and. branding cycle reduces the reputation of a business by just only one word or phrase. It is said that the American Marketing Association describes a branding as the name, a term mark, logo or design, or any combination of them, that is designed to differentiate and distinguish between the items or services offered by the competition of a single retailer or group of retailers.' Brand Equity is the name of the brand's value due to its long-standing reputation and trustworthiness which results in more sales and higher profits than other brands in the marketplace. Internal branding is a crucial element of strategic planning in the creation of brand equity. When implementing a brand campaign an authority in marketing or contractor considers four different perspectives to develop an effective branding-consumer view (to evaluate the appeal of the product or service for a range of customers) The Perspective from the Company (to improvethe technical or aesthetically, presentation, and the third). Branding is the person you are when you promote your brand and impact the decision-making of consumers. This is why the purpose of brand management or branding is the marketing process which involves the evaluation and development of the brand's position on the marketplace, which is directed towards the general public and the protection of a suitable brand's reputation. A business or an entrepreneur advertises their products or services to prospective customers through advertisements. The term "advertisement" is used to describe "Any type of pay-per-click communication." Most popular marketing outlets are press and digital, as well as, and social media. The concept of marketing is that it is the strategy or method used to convince prospective buyers to purchase the appropriate product or service. Advertising translates strategies for marketing into various media. It informs potential buyers in advertisements that they've got the correct product or service. The main issue of nowadays is the overwhelming. Cluttering. Cluttering. "The clutter is the amount of advertising messages to which the customer is constantly exposed on a daily basis." The primary responsibility of marketing professionals is to control the mess. It is difficult to determine the ideal time to speak with customers you want to reach and providing the best feedback regarding your company's situation.

Marketing is different from. Networking The concept of networking is one that involves a system human interaction with other people. Networking in the corporate world is always linked to efficient marketing. Corporate networking is a result of the socio-economic experiences of entrepreneurs. It is a circle of corporate networks. It is important to note that A business circle is part of the larger socio-economic circle that an entrepreneur has. If there isn't a proper collaboration among all economic players / shareholders, a business be unsuccessful or fail at the very least to its fullest potential. To build an efficient business network, managers and colleagues from a broad socio-economic circle are vital. The secret to successful marketing lies in networking BtoB as well as BtoC.

Effective marketing includes branding, networking, advertising sales and promotion. Networking places consumers in ' areas, while branding allows for changing standards or reshaping customer interactions. Advertisements communicate the message through various products or services. Marketing encourages consumers to purchase and ultimately the profit from the transaction is realized.

What is the criteria for a prospective who is Qualified?

Have you ever thought about what the key characteristics of a prospective prospect? What are the most important requirements I must be aware of to determine whether there is a marketing opportunity? What information is necessary to identify the right potential customer?

Do I follow an efficient sales process or system to collect the information I need efficiently? The 17 categories that you can inquire about your own needs to build a professional prospect profile . This is known by the name of an account profile.

You should ask yourself "What kind of company should I select when selling?" Do you have a company that has 10 employees or 100 employees? Does the business have gross sales that exceed 10 million dollars or gross revenues in excess of $100 million?

Are the majority of my customers clients from the financial or retail industries? What types of businesses give the most money as compensation for short time for sales?

In short, what are some of the traits of your most competitive...

The Total Group sales section Complete Number of employees Goods, Services or Systems for business practices . How is the account currently operating? • Industries Verticals (e.g. Technology and printers, frozen food and more.)

Where is Mr. Prospect?

What is it that Mrs. Prospect been up to previously?

What is the strategy of Mr. Prospect?

Where would Mrs. Prospect be?

What does Mr. Prospect attempting to get there?

Problems, needs, or challenges crucial business problems, challenges or drivers are your solutions perceived or not?

What is Mrs. Prospect's hopes, fears or issues?

Who is responsible for their care?

What are the steps needed to resolve the problem? Does this fit with your solution?

Will Mr. Prospect actively seek out solutions that you might give him?

Does Mrs. Prospect know of any commercial plans that are currently in progress or planned for the in the near future?

Are Mr. Prospect curious about what you can provide?

Does Mrs. Prospect be required to resolve an urgent business problem?

Was Mr. Prospect using outdated items and/or services, which may need to be replaced?

Do you think a specific product or service needed however Mrs. Prospect cannot afford to design her own solution over many hours or even money?

Does Mr. Prospect employ a solution but not get business outcomes?

Will Mrs. Prospect start looking at her competitors?

What is the best way for a person to come up with a solution for an issue?

Do you think Mr. Prospect serious about buying or are they simply an unnecessary waste of time or tire kickers or simply a way to get me some thing?

Time frames. What are time frames to serve...

Evaluation Period RFI, RFP or RFP or (Requests for information proposal, proposals or quotes) The date of the Evaluation Period of roll-out of A pilot solution for business-wide budget for implementation of the solution Mr. Prospects budgeted?

Would Mrs. Prospect obtain it from a different project or even from the budget in the coming year?

At what point do further sign-offs required? ($10,000, $50,000? $100,000) What can you estimate the value of the solution?

Do you have a time-limit for Mr. Potential to lose his funding or budget (usually in government and school organisations)?

The right fit is your solution is a good fit for your business?

Do we need to maintain a relationship?

Have you analyzed how much return on investment (Investment Return)?

How long is the Net Payback time and how easy can the solution be paid?

Have you come up with an argument for cost (time cost or the time saved)?

What can get them smiling?

Is Mr. Prospect's company growing or is it in trouble?

Have you purchased the vision or solution suggested?

Can our strategy aid Mrs. Prospect realize real ROI estimates?

Are the services and products currently being used or are additional products or services required?

Does Mr. Prospect ready to take specific steps to solve the issue?

Criteria for evaluation What's the criteria to be evaluated, if any? Do they intend to send it to you electronically?

Are you able to provide a standard using which you can provide them?

What are the factors that influenced this final choice?

Are there any agreements regarding what's important or valuable?

Are the standards for assessment set?

Business Impact What are the consequences of error or inaction?

If the account isn't able to respond by a specific date What do you mean by penalties or consequences?

What is the cost to lose a client?

How much will it cost to purchase a customer?

What would an increase in headcount cost?

What is the cost of removing your shopping cart on your online shop?

What's the price for additional training? Also, how much time are you spending in training?

Did you take into account the impact on your business?

What will Mrs. Prospect stand to gain or lose in the event that a solution is implemented or not?

Mechanisms What exactly are the mechanisms for assessing, budgeting and decision-making?

Who's going to be the one to negotiate?

What compromises can be made What is a compromise, and what should not be resolved?

Who is the person who signs on the Final Accord?

What are the terms of the payment (Net 15, Net 30, etc.)?

Do you need to buy an order?

Who will take part or influence any final decisions?

It could be one person or a different.

Are there people (or or an entity) who is aware of the benefits for your service or product but hasn't yet found a suitable match?

Are all the principal players identified and were they contacted?

Are you speaking with the right person, and do you are able to purchase if you have the right solution?

Do you know what authority Mr. Prospect has to be able to get further approvals?

What are their decision makers, appraisers influencers, and the end-users?

Final Judgment This report is made by the Maker(s).

Motivation: What's the effect on us?

The assessor(s) screens and states"no. Motivation: What is the most effective solution to our situation?

Guide(s) will assist in guiding the operation.

Motivation: Your idea I appreciate. How can I assist you in deciding on your next step?

End users are concerned about the effects they have on their work and.

Motivation What will make my job more or less difficult?

The initiator(s) wants to appear attractive.

Motivation: How do show that I've conducted a thorough research?

Conditions and terms of contracts, legal or purchase must be agreed upon.

Motivation: How do you achieve the most favorable conditions (i.e. more promotions, extra technical support, or other requirements) in terms of client service of consultation, less expensive cost, additional training, more documentation, better terms for the payment and warranties and so on.)?

How formal or informal is your company?

Who should be reported to whom? Who does the filing?

Who has an impact on who? Who is a factor in who?

Who are their co-workers, backups or colleagues?

Who are the people who help?

Did you spell the correct titles and names?

Are you provided with your correct address for the street and email addresses, fax numbers and extensions (room or suite, floor mail code, etc.)?

Which of your contacts ' responsibility?

What kinds of services and products are currently in use?

Are the candidates equipped with the time, resources and equipment required to put the solution into location or readily available?

The right climate could be created to encourage your plan?

Competitors What other firms are thinking about, and why? Competition

Which is the one that prefers to follow the other company and why?

What do you think? Do you love or dislike Mrs. Prospect's new supplier?

What is on the list If Mr. Prospect had a wishlist and could get or might have something he wanted from either his current or a potential supplier?

Locations Are the decisions made hierarchically (a single location is the sole authority for the entire location) as well as decentralized (each area decides for itself)?

How many branches, sites or partnerships? and/or joint ventures do you have, and with whom?

Would you consider promoting your solution in a broad manner instead of a departmental and business unit-based basis?

Are there any other locations that are your customers, partners or affiliates?

Is Mr. Prospect confidence in you?

Have you earned credibility?

Are Mrs. Prospect fully aware of the business?

Does Mr. Prospect really believe you're taking action in the best interest?

Does Mrs. Prospect be confident in the capability of your company to assist her and provide to solve your problem?

Ressources Does Mr. Prospect have the required time and resources to conduct an assessment?

Does Mrs. Prospect have enough time and resources required to create an expense justification?

Does Mr. Prospect have a strategy or access to funds for discretionary use available?

Does Mrs. Prospect be able to convey your ideas within the correct physical surroundings?

What are the primary requirements that you must meet for your item or service?

After you have summarized your discussion After completing your summary, you should follow up on the next steps: "What is next?" (or "What's what's the next thing to do?" "Where do we next go?" "If we can find solutions that are better than the one you have chosen What is the process you're taking to look at alternatives?" "What should we take to get moving?"

Have you set up the sales M.A.P. (Mutual Process Agreement (TM))?

What is the best time and day for these tasks?

What is the timeline and what are the steps to take to finish the sale?

The next steps need to be specific about the time and date. "Next month, I'll contact you to follow up" doesn't mean "Next Tuesday at 3pm Eastern Time we're going to discuss the advantages of the idea after having been able to discuss the idea with your colleagues, is it?"

How to Enhance your Call to Action

The website was stunning, but it didn't have any results. Sure, visitors visited the website, but no one phoned, and no one placed an order. The problem wasn't the page's traffic. The issue was not pricing. The site's performance issues were principally due to the website's call to take action. The thing that made the website's call to action so shabby was not how it appeared or was read and the minuscule results it generated. Enhancing the call to action and making it easier when you know what you need to do, will significantly improve the performance of your website. Let's look at the most important aspects to improve the performance of your site or increase sales by determining what's not working with your call to actions.

The importance of calling for actions is vital, but it's a technique that's underrated for convincing and selling, which can produce disappointing results in the worst scenario when relying on it. If you want someone to do something, you need to solicit it directly. Your public is eagerly awaiting it. Don't let them down. Don't be a nuisance to them. That is, if you'd like someone to contact you, inform them to contact you - and give them a great excuse.

A good call for action can result in results. It's more than just giving someone a directive to do something. It's about asking for the right answer and in the right manner and at the right moment. Let's take a look at how this process works.

The appropriateness of your call to action actually means that you have to ensure that the action you want to take is appropriate. Think of the purchase as the result of a process. First, we acknowledge the need, and then search for information, which is and then we look at the options, leading to buying, and we review the purchase. Your request for action must be suitable for the format and the stage of the purchasing procedure. To begin an auto dealer may invite customers to visit and take a look at the cars that are they have on their property. If someone shows an the interest for a particular vehicle and the dealer has determined that it's a viable possibility, he is invited to take the vehicle for the test drive. The invitation to test drive of the car is not open to everyone; it is open to those who decide to take the next reasonable and appropriate step in their purchasing decision. That is, different requests for action are made at various dates and times are dependent on the needs of prospective buyers and desires.

The most common error here is that the demand to action is not enough for attention and trust that was previously established. I generally view it as an invitation to an action, which is essentially an appeal to "buy right now" however it's better to ask for action, which provides more details, thus establishing trust and being more responsive to the needs of the buyer at that particular moment.

I can see a good call to action occasionally however it's hard to locate it on the site. It should be easily accessible in order to be successful. That is you should offer your actions on your site, not only on a couple of pages. Nowadays most sites are powered by design. Therefore, you can add your call-to-action to the various page templates you've created on your website. If you do this, you will be able to ensure that it is displayed consistently across your site, based on your specific page templates. Nearly all pages on your website must contain a call to action.

The location of the appropriate call-to-action is dependent on its appropriateness. The main issue is that you might need more than one kind of call-to-action to achieve optimal results, so that you can provide an item that is crucial for the customer in the purchasing decision. For example, when you make the call to action the contact can be equivalent. It could be a phone number, E-mail address, a contact form, instant chat or chat. This kind of information should be on the pages that you would like to talk with you directly via your website.

When a page is plausible to anticipate, however not yet ready for direct communication to anyone who would need more details The most important thing could be calling to action. This could be in form in the form of a download or an application delivered via postal mail.

The placement of the relevant information also implies that, based on the potential customer's interests, you might require different versions of the call to move. For instance, a lawyer might have a manual or a report specifically regarding wills and estate planning as well as on starting a business. The proper location of the will as well as the estate planning file must be on the web pages on this subject and also for downloading the business initial. Relevance has a lot to determine what you can reasonably expect from your.

Expectations Customers have specific expectations of your website. The effectiveness of your site through increasing the number in leads as well as sales that you get from it has a lot about operating within and in line with the guidelines. Making your call to action to meet your visitors' expectations can significantly boost the number of visitors who respond to the call to action you have made after visiting your site.

Social Proof Social proof provides an evidence of the actions of other people. It is not a good idea to make arbitrary choices. People's instincts and the mentality of the group are prevalent. When making a choice, we want to look at what other people are doing. This isn't just for the political system, and a lot of people feel more confident by looking at what other people have accomplished. It's not enough just to inform people to be careful. It is essential to demonstrate. You have to demonstrate it. That's why it's known as "cultural factual evidence." This type of proof can be in the form of case studies, testimonials white papers, etc. The more personal details you include, the more effectiveness and power of your testimonial. It is recommended to include a picture of your the first and last names and the location. But for certain industries it is not feasible. For instance, clients of a defense lawyer are not likely to supply evidence that includes such data. In some cases, clients cannot offer testimonials or private information. In other cases, professional boards and licensing boards could limit the contents of their testimony.

For example, your testimony may focus on your client service, not the outcomes or the results (think the economic consultant you worked with. The evidence may only contain the names of the person as well as the state and city of his residence. Remember, there's always a way of proving the facts. It can be difficult to imagine.

Credibility, the end result that comes from using the social evidence properly will be that the credibility of your will be enhanced, and people feel more at ease with them. If you're able to engage in the conversation from your own perspective your credibility will be increased. It's not as mysterious as it sounds. It is a natural process in the event that you are able to identify your target audience well. You can customize the message to appeal to your audience by knowing the needs of your customers to make sure that it resonates with them. This improves confidence and will make the company significantly more secure.

A credible product has to be reliable for the audience you're targeting. It should have a purpose. It should reflect something your ideal view is attracted to when you present it. Any commitments or statements that you make, whether they are implicit or explicit, must be viewed by your target audience as trustworthy. This can mean reaffirming the assertion to increase its credibility. Sometimes, it is sensible to make promises and deliver.

The right approach is amazing and easily accessible as is the incentive that comes by your request to act. The absence of the other will only produce modest results. The advantage of increasing your call to action is that it will make the same amount of visitors to your site immediately more productive. Imagine the profits increasing without having to spend more money.

Turning your Qualified Prospect into a Customer

You cannot think that your sales goals will be consistently exceeded unless you discover how to make maximum use of your day every day. It is a scarce resource that can keep you in the same position for a long time by investing it in the right way to get extraordinary results and when it is spent. The process of continuing to pursue any prospect or lead can be as effective as screaming about a looming tornado and demanding it disappear. If you don't follow through then you'll just go through the day circling around in circles and you may even pay however, most of the time you're just wasting your time and gain little.

It can be difficult to evaluate prospects or leads when you're not 100% sure of the service you can offer or the benefits prospects can benefit. You cannot sort out lead or prospective leads that are viable and decide which you'll invest your time and effort to convert into clients if you do not know whether what you are offering is beneficial to them in the first. Make clear what you are offering and explain the benefits you can offer your customers and you will save yourself hours each day of searching through possible prospects and qualification. The effort you put into it and ultimately leads to qualification, saves you time and effort since you'll only spend your money with the right people who are in need of exactly what you have to offer.

Prospects are similar to you. They also have a limited amount of time, and don't want to spend your time trying to convince them of something that's not suitable for their requirements. It is important to understand the details and whether your value proposition is able to accomplish the job. If you're properly prepared and are aware of precisely what your value proposition is and how it will benefit the customers, they'll soon realize your expertise as confident, and they'll eventually begin to trust your business. It is a fact that customers buy, appreciate and trust people they trust. It is impossible to trust or love an individual who is unexperienced or doesn't know and who is willing to create your own opinion.

Convert qualified pathways into sales Opportunities and pathways that qualify. Qualified pathways are the engine that powers the sales engine, and ultimately drives the revenue of any business. Any sales professional that wants to surpass sales goals every day must be diligently researching every prospect till they are able to have a precise idea of what their requirements for the future are and how the value proposition can meet these and also how they can communicate with the prospect and build an enlightened connection with the prospect. The more prepared you are prior to any sales call and the more you understand the purpose of each sales phone call, the more your prospects will be prepared and will be able to warm you up and more enthusiastically accept your offer.

In the words of Everett Rogers, who published an article titled "Dispersion of creativity' and the transformation of your Qualified Prospect into a consumer and an actual client goes through five distinct phases: awareness, interest as well as follow-up. The final stage is acceptance. Your knowledge of your offer's value and the work you've completed on the requirements of the person who is the decision maker puts you in a strong position to move your prospect from that you are aware of your value proposition to a point at which you actually want to accept or purchase your service or product.

It's creating awareness. If you have the client you have carefully chosen because it is perfect for the services you offer. There is no better method to get in touch with them than by presenting your personal and worth proposition face-to-face calls. If you are aware that this isn't always possible as decision makers typically have porters that make it extremely difficult to get to know them. That's why you need to think a bit more creative and utilize every instrument to get them to know about you and your unique value proposition.

Action Idea: Making use of social media is a great method of connecting with potential prospects. The trick to making this work for yourself is not trying to sell anything via social media. If you try to market your service or product via any platform on social media, it is rejected or ignored completely. Social media is about sharing and sharing, therefore you should first get in touch with the person on Facebook, LinkedIn, or Twitter to make use of this platform effectively.

Once you've agreed to the connection request, take a examine it and discover ways to share it and offer content compatible with your interests or interests, or anything else you'd like to get connected with. When they've met that you're trustworthy Ask them what they've done throughout their life time. People are fond of talking about themselves and they'll share their personal information, that will be useful as you go on as you establish your relationship.

Everyone is curious and once you have explained what you do and what they do in return, they'll ask the same question. When asked what you're doing you shouldn't get out of the way and attempt to convince them. Be careful and remain somewhat shady and yet provide them with enough information to make them interested. It is possible to request an appointment or phone conversation as you begin asking specific questions about what you're doing and giving them information. We know that have a lot to prove, and we are not sure about your business and are interested in what you have to accomplish. You've basically brought them to the next stage of deciding on your product or service since they are curious about the work you're doing.

How to accomplish this Evaluation and Review Once you change from being interested to knowledge then the next step is to evaluate. This is the moment to remove any risk from your view. You have confidence in the product or service you offer and have thoroughly studied and evaluated your prospects and provide them with a 100 percent money-back guarantee, which carries the least amount of risk. This, however suggests that you trust in your work enough that you're willing to share it with others in the event that it doesn't do what you expect it to do. This removes any risk from the potential clients and allows them to be confident in what you are required to provide.

After examining or evaluating your products, buyers will recognize the high quality of your products and they will be able to purchase when they purchase from your. This strategy is only feasible when you are confident in your product and are confident in the product you're selling. The confidence you place in what you sell is essential to achieving sales success If you don't believe that buyers will buy the product you sell for the amount you offer, you will not always succeed in selling it.

Chapter 8: Surviving A Market That Is Hard

Market

Deja vu is defined by Webster's Collegiate Dictionary: something that is overly or unsettlingly familiar. Anyone who worked in the industry of staffing during the latter half of the 1980s to early 1990s is aware precisely what this refers to in relation to the wages of employees. Prior to the start of the 1980s no one was concerned about the price of compensation, or the effects of rollercoaster primes.

There weren't any terms like "soft market" or "hard market" however the cost of wages of workers began to go up to the mid-point of the late 1980s. As the trend accelerated numerous firms were forced to rely in self-insurance or retention programs, or other forms of alternative insurance. Everyone was aware that the State account or risk pool allocated to staffing companies was a death sentence for a company that specialized in staffing. However, around the mid 90s the market began to plummet without warning. Companies that had previously quit the insurance market in search of alternative insurance options realize that the cost from a cash flow standpoint of compensation for workers through traditional methods is much more attractive. Many companies have requested employees to pay for their services and enjoyed the price war. Industries are quoted rates that are significantly lower than the earlier times. Changers were not considered or discussed and, despite some exceptions, premium credit were the standard. There was not much discussion on the risk management process of a business. There was a great need for the carriers supply.

The reasoning behind this soft market was that companies recognized and dealt with injuries-related issues. In the United States, losses fell and many believed that the market will never be "hard" ever again. In the process of requesting an insurance quote, the insurers did not pay consideration to the insurance company's attitude towards protection and damage control. While there are some reasons for the weak market, but they aren't the primary motives. To be able to survive in a difficult market, it is essential to understand the reasons behind why it happens. If you don't know the factors that drive an economy that is either hard or soft the business could be unable to make a difference and survive.

Let's first consider the steps taken by businesses when their insurance costs began increase. Numerous companies began looking at ways to reduce their costs. In the beginning of 1990 they observed that insurers would offer higher rates in exchange for an amount of their losses. The higher the retention rate, the higher rates they would offer. This means the insured need to increase their security and risk control procedures to ensure the deductibles (retention rates) are maintained to the minimum. A lot of attention was given to the development of thorough processes to identify employees that could be injured or who could file fraudulent claims. Employees were provided with additional safety education. Drug screening has become well-known, and many companies have employed or assigned risk managers, regardless of whether they're qualified. A new way of evaluating customers was introduced, and a group effort was created between employees and their clients to improve security and decrease losses. The result was an enormous reduction in loss ratios that drew to the attention of a range of insurance companies.

Many companies of the time were not willing to issue benefits insurance for employees for their employees due to the fact that they were of the opinion that they could control the workplace or worker and their workplace. The data of the past supported the notion. It is important to remember that this was the time when the majority of people thought workplace organizations as "secretarial swimming pools" or "lent an alcoholic." But, with losses that were 150 percent or more the losses were far greater than the amount of premiums paid. Therefore, who is to blame insurance companies for not accepting this type of insurance? Given the intense risk management carried out along with a number of months of successes, which resulted in lower or 35% losses, and a portion of the losses being recouped, the chance of success by providing that insurance companies were able to meet their requirements increased. Consequently, certain companies took the risk of taking on this type of insurance.

However, good methods of risk management weren't the only reason to safeguard a well-known high-risk sector. When you look at the chart of the market over the last 10 years, you will quickly see that the connection between the market for shares as well as the market for insurance is there. Therefore. This is why. Insurance companies collect the cost of premiums from their customers, but they do not settle claims. This is generally for a time before they pay the claims. They can put the money into investments and earn the return. If the rates are reasonable as well as the return is high insurers are more concerned with the amount they own rather than their value to the person they are insuring. For instance, the insurance industry suffered losses of 4 billion dollars in one year. (That seems like a lot however it's a small amount.) Thirty-four billion dollars in investment income was reported in the same year. With a total of thirty billion, it's clear the reason why regardless of risk they'd prefer premium funds. In reality that the pendulum has been swinging towards the opposite direction to the point where that companies might, in a lot of instances, be able to obtain the commitment pricing method at a lower cost than the retention plan. This is a temporary situation and, when interest rates dropped and the market started its downward slide it returned to the pendulum in a rapid manner.

Another factor to consider is the frequency of events occurring in the course of a year. The impact of floods, hurricanes tornadoes, earthquakes, fire and droughts on all types of insurance premiums. A lot of insurance companies are restricted to a single type of coverage, such as salaries for employees. We typically have a range in coverage column. If these disasters hit the carriers in a severe way or they lose millions of dollars in job instances, like discrimination, it could impact the cost of premiums in all ways. The losses from catastrophic events were not as severe until the middle of the 90s. If a company suffers losses to the extent that they need to close every insurer has an impact. The fall of Universal Re is an example of this. When the company was forced to cease operations due to poor underwriting, the prices soared almost instantly across the nation between 5% and 20%, and other reinsurance companies scrambled to defend themselves from the same situation. A majority of front-line carriers either faced financial difficulties or saw their position plummet significantly.

A number of insurance experts began to warn about the possibility of a rough market in 1998. The economy was still booming however, the prices were still very low, and advisories dropped dramatically. They realized that investments would not yield large returns. It was also evident that firms became comfortable with their risk management procedures. With the possibility of a disastrous year, businesses were warned of the impending hard market. And it did in the same way that experts predicted.

For some, it's too for them to save their business because insurance companies have turned their backs on employees and profits have been wiped out through the steep costs in workers' compensation that are a part of the State Fund or assigned risk pool. Certain companies have already closed their doors, and others have offered their companies to larger corporations for lower prices than what they actually are worth. There are many more to come until this market gets over.

After you have a better understanding of the factors that cause the fluctuations in the economy What do you do to remain afloat and prevent a loss from happening again? In the first place, you must establish a long-term perspective to planning , rather than "insurance carrier jumping." Insurance companies are seeking companies that are looking to form long-term relationships as well as the ones which spring every year. This kind of relationship helps the insurer comprehend the requirements of the insured more effectively and gain from the typical. Every business is at risk of having a poor year. A bad year may be more successful than good ones on average. When you form a bond with a company and stay to it for a specific period of time, they will benefit both. Be aware that the price isn't crucial; the costs are very high. If the company offers poor service, a small initial cost could end up costing you thousands of dollars. This could be due to inadequate treatment of complaints or poor report of the secret exclusions. No matter who is responsible the ability of you to obtain low-cost insurance can negatively impact the year's high-risk loss. Take action immediately, if that's the case in your present situation!

If you can you should consider a certain amount of retention. You are accountable for the first-rate dollar claims and you are required to minimize or eliminate a significant portion of these claims. It is important to note that the company is required to pay $1.50 to $2.00 per dollar. You could save between 50 and 100 percent on this part of the case after you've paid the first cent. Be sure that the contract you signed prevents the company in charging for the costs. The amount of retention is available in a range of sizes and, as they grow you should consider that the business must provide security in the shape of credit letter or cash. This could have disastrous consequences for production and cash flow. The most well-known rate of retention was 10,000, 50,000 100,000, 250,000 and between 500,000 and 1 million dollars for larger businesses. Captive and Rent-a-Captive plans are very beneficial since they enable you to communicate more effectively and usually offer a refund of a part of your costs following a lower loss year. A lot of these plans provide investment income dollars, which is usually paid to the provider. Yet lookout. It is essential to be aware of the way these programs function prior to transferring. These kinds of services are likely to be suited for business owners with long-term plans and a solid strategy to limit losses. If this type of approach is not available in the system you're contemplating, you should steer clear of it. The captive services will require more cash in advance, however the longer-term advantages could significantly lower the cost of insurance. Since they are not as susceptible to cash flow problems at the beginning and therefore, it is crucial to examine your financial standing prior to registering for this kind of program.

If you are considering a particular plan, it's better to get the assistance of an independent third-party professional prior to deciding. This is because the choice won't be influenced by a consultant in determining the fee an agent, broker or a different direct writer might receive. One company that took this approach recently paid modest amount to consultants to examine the broker's proposal. After careful examination consulting experts were able determine areas that were more suitable to the insured while in conjunction with the broker. The study resulted into an increase of 48% in the renewal rate of the company. The cost for consulting was one percent. This represents an average savings of 47. It's not your case however it doesn't need to be a good thing to discuss.

Then, take a moment to go over the risk management plan. Analytical analysis will uncover areas that have been neglected because of absence of focus. Changes in the situation mean that it is possible to upgrade or eliminate other components of your system in order to better meet the requirements of your customer. Sometimes, the expense of a security procedure is weighed against the results. If the cost is higher than the benefit, you can opt not to use this approach. Look for ways to ease managing risk for your employees, and keep in mind that they're following your model. You cannot expect your employees to behave differently if you don't stick to your plan. Give them the right tools and make the accountable inability to implement a risk management system that is effective. It is important to ensure that a company who is considering a quote for your company and decides to visit your facility proves that you're a safe risk. Don't be expecting them to accept your claim just because you've read an entire book on risk management and handful of forms. There have been times when they've done this, but they will not be the next victim of this kind of practice. Make risk management a routine component of your program. This will result in fewer costs for injuries and more savings on insurance renewal.

If you stick to these basic guidelines and pay attention to the elements like the market's volatility and the impact of catastrophic events, you will be able to survive in a tough market, and prosper in a calm market.

Marketing Your Idea

If I receive inquiries from inventors for due diligence I prefer to provide a brief illustration of this. If a business was ready to design the product, manufacture it, and then sell it the new product which could likely cost between $50,000 and $150,000 to create, plus production costs, they will certainly decide to take the time to make the right business decision and take the product to market (i.e. they have conducted an inquiry about products). It is possible to consider 'due diligence' to be the method of obtaining all the information needed to make a sound business decision prior to spending huge sums of money. In theory, the more time, energy and money (i.e., "risk") the company has to invest in the pursuit of innovation and generating new ideas, the higher the potential license will be estimated.

Remember that, even if an idea appears to be simple and affordable however, the process of development and production isn't always easy and affordable. Companies must consider various factors, including feedback from customers as well as retail price points, production unit cost, the competitive environments, potential market growth, manufacturing viability and more.

This is based on the strategy you've selected to promote your brand.

If you plan to develop and market the product yourself it will require due diligence. In reality, you are the inventor of the product and, consequently, must take the same care when developing your invention just like other manufacturing company. What I've observed is the fact that a lot of inventors who decide to make their own inventions. If they are any this is a serious error.

Option 2: Licensing royalty--if you are planning to license royalties I'm assuming you'll need to cut down on your due diligence because they'll conduct its own due diligence prior to any company licenses your invention. If you are working with a company like Invention Home and Invention Home, your invention is likely to cost businesses a minimal amount. It could cost more than simply selling your idea to businesses (which is in essence the best method of due diligence). Be aware that you must have taken the time to conduct your market research, as well as a patent search earlier to ensure that you're going after your product in the first place (i.e. you are ensuring that your product isn't available and that there is a market).

Let me sum up. If you're looking to invest a substantial amount of money into your invention, be sure to first determine if it's worth it. If you can promote your invention effectively within companies with a low cost, you will be certain that a interested business will conduct its due diligence (do not trust yourself). Be aware that it is important to have data available on due diligence for advertising when analyzing the possibilities of innovation with potential companies but this information isn't always easy to acquire, so it is important to weigh the expense and effort involved in data collection against the actual requirements.

As mentioned, the aim of due diligence in advertising is to gather the most information possible and to determine the best way the best time to invest in any item. I'll also give you some tips for due diligence. We'd have all of the required information in the ideal world of forecasts for sales and marketing costs, retail prices production setup and cost of units, competitive analysis and market demand. It isn't always readily available but it is possible.

You can do the research yourself even if you're not able to hire a reputable company to perform your analysis of your advertisement but you should know that research must be used and viewed as a whole and should not be considered to be of high quality. What you do with the data. It is important to note to not conduct "Market research" from innovators who are promoting inventions. The idea is sometimes promoted as an "first first step" these figures are generally useless since it's not a thorough study regarding your invention (usually with a high-priced "advertising" software). Instead, it's "canned" business figures from the shelf that won't aid you in making an informed decision.

Before we move on to"the "tips," I should mention the concept of "due diligence" can be described under a variety of names. Due diligence * Marketing Assessment* Innovation salabilityProfitably economicmarket research* Evaluation of inventions These terms are primarily used to describe research that examines the potential of the productivity and salary of an invention. It's impossible to say that with certainty whether the invention is going to be sold, however you can know the odds of its success more thoroughly.

Also, if you are planning to develop your invention on your own take into consideration doing due diligence marketing on your concept. The entity that has approved your invention will perform the work if you want licensing your innovation in exchange for royalty.

A few ideas for due diligence marketing are listed below.

1. Find out the most fundamental questions. Is your idea truly original or has someone else already had the idea already? If you're doing your own study, you've already completed

this task. If not, you can search the commercial folders or internet.

Does your idea provide a solution to a problem? solution? If not, then why do you think that it will be a success?

Do you have a solution to the problem that is based on your idea?

Are your ideas available for sale? If so, what do the competition offer your invention?

How many competitors and other competitors can you identify?

What is the range of prices for these items? Do you think your brand could be included in the range? Be sure to avail of the benefits and possibly royalty and wholesale costs If there are any.

Can you better position your invention?

2. List the advantages and disadvantages of how your invention sells, and evaluate your list objectively-Demand-Is your invention demand present?

Market-does the product you are selling have an audience, and if then, what's the magnitude of the demand?

Production capabilities- will your invention be simple or challenging to make?

Costs for manufacturing-can you provide exact production cost estimates (both per unit, and for the tooling and installation)?

Distribution Capabilities - Is selling or distributing your invention easy or complicated?

Advanced features - do you significantly boost your product's innovation when compared with other similar products (speed or weight, volume, etc.)? ?

Retail Price-do you have gained or lost from an established price?

Is your product going to last longer than the other products?

Performance: Does your invention perform best (including higher, more rapid outputs, quieter or odor, taste appearance, or feel) over other products?

Are there market barriers that make getting into your market difficult or simple?

Do your innovations comply with laws and regulations? need or require special laws to be followed or have unique regulations (i.e., FDA approval) 3. Search for advice or input from others (confidentiality consideration)- Professional / field experts target.

Goal-related inputs and Guidance inquiry.

Meet with professional marketers.

For sales representatives who are on-site.

Let people know who you meet.

Contact family and friends members whom you can trust.

Get their input regarding the invention like the advantages, features prices, features, and whether they would be willing to purchase the product.

During the process of inspection the current producers gain from the ability to talk to their buyers (retail purchasers, wholesalers etc.). My opinion is that one of the most crucial elements for a business is whether the existing customers purchase the product. I'd want to patent my product if I could sell an idea to a company (if they were able to make it at a reasonable price) in the event that a major customer agreed to purchase the product.

It's a major driver for businesses considering licensing their products regardless of whether a consumer would like to purchase the product. She observed a variety of scenarios that showed businesses intrigued by an ingenuous idea concept, but they decided to drop the idea due to not attracted by the product of their customers (the retail store). On the other hand, she noticed businesses that had a slight enthusiasm for the idea of the market if the retailer is interested in the product.

The breakdown of Sales and Marketing

Reviving the sales and marketing discussion. Back in October we posted a piece that was titled "5 strategies that marketing departments can employ can use to help salespeople catch Butterfly." A 10-fold writing piece was recently published, with the title "What's the core of marketing and sales, and what are their benefits?." What is the reason you are now rethinking this? Because the link between marketing and sales has never been more obvious than now, in particular due to advances in the field of marketing technology.

Many people in the business world particularly those who are that are dependent on the performance of marketing and sales aren't really equipped with an understanding of what marketing and sales are. They are interconnected but they're not exactly the identical. Marketing is dependent on sales departments There are also departments of marketing as well as feeding strategies for sales (note that I didn't declare that I was "making" revenue). If you didn't have anything of value to offer, you could not engage in the advertising process, which means your sales strategies will be less educated and effective without your marketing efforts. Yes, the majority of top people in sales (or push-pickers) can generate businesses on their own, and may even resort to sleeping in their beds with tried and tested strategies for marketing, but they're not equipped with the skills, resources or tools to leverage their potential market.

A common error that is made by more established, bigger businesses is believing that salespeople are skilled in advertising and that marketers are sales trained. It may be true in some instances however it's not true all the time. Many businesses try to mix their marketing and sales teams in order to save money , and they mainly employ their employees in two job descriptions. it is generally a bad choice. It's not an accident that businesses that are newly established as well as technology companies and companies that hire a lot of young people, fail through their marketing strategies.

How to break it down As we discussed in the post on tenfolds about building relationships, the next step to closing retention is just one of the most important sales team duties: the chance to maintain a relationship that is private. Many customers that have purchased from the exact dealer, brand or trade show for decades will admit that they appreciate the personal attention given to them. It's not a marketing department's responsibility to monitor the existing customer's business following the lead's announcement or revealed. It is also not their job to convert a lead into a sale, "close the deal" or make sure that the client is a customer for many the next few years. The primary factors that aid in customer retention include an outstanding rapport with a knowledgeable salesperson, high-quality product and an overall great satisfaction.

Marketing efforts are of prime importance. They are a contribution to conscience to transformation (from anonymous to well-known) retention. This isn't the duty of the salesperson to create awareness the awareness of their product, brand or service. If you're supposed to utilize your resources to create sales by developing leads and connections, how do you possibly expect time to perform the work that eventually brings you buyers to your table?

The marketing department educates and communicates by creating content that stimulates people to take action, targets and monitors the engagement of the user by urging individuals to supply contact information or request an unrestricted trial or a consultation (which converts people from being cold to a well-known prospect or a potential buyer). It is crucial to remember that the role of a marketing department in retention is not a substitute for the retention efforts of sales teams.

On the selling side, the retention of customers is much more heavily to salespeople's ability to make use of the relationship with customers to continuously evaluate the business, and try to get them involved in ongoing discussions about potential products or services that are of their interest, and to get suggestions from family and friends members of the customer. But loyalty in the marketing department is based on maintaining a higher degree of involvement (through targeted marketing that is based on buying preferences, preferences and past experiences) to ensure that the relationship with the customer does not be over after the first purchase. These updates that you get after becoming customers aren't just randomly-- they have an intention and are often in response to the information you've read or expressed interest in. A sales team certainly isn't equipped with the knowledge and time, nor the resources to execute strategic strategies like this.

The perfect coexistence of It All The ideal relationship between marketing and sales is synergistic. Both parties work to figure out what the consumer wants and the best way to meet their needs. Marketing and sales should empower, encourage and feeding each other. They must work in tandem and be able to coexist. Marketing and sales shouldn't be seen as rivals or even equal partners in the company food chain rather, subordinates. They are not able to survive in isolation from the others, however their capabilities are not the same- particularly in the present, when technology advances demand an extensive, highly specific set of competencies for the modern marketer which salespeople don't require.

That's why the majority of marketers, researchers and introverts are sensible people. If you're Numbers analysing and reviewing data, analyzing trends and conversion rate reports or writing excellent advertisements and designing great collateral materials and websites It is essential to focus on what's happening and what's not going on and make changes to your creative approach. The marketing department should generally contain people who are innovative analysts, analysts, and technologically oriented (who get lost in the math and algorithms behind the sophisticated marketing tools).

Yet, many salespeople are extroverts. They brighten up the room, possess amazing "people abilities," can easily connect with other people, and find out information that could aid them in making an agreement.

Salespeople also concentrate more on, not just being at a desk doing the things that marketing departments do best, which is to fill their time in meetings and other events. The majority of salespeople employ administrative assistants to help them with their supervision, paperwork and scheduling, phone calls or proposals, as well as scheduling. This type of position as an operational assistant in the field of marketing isn't as prevalent.

How to Market and Close Your Way to Millions of Dollars in MLM

Super-Rich MLM Gurus' ideas The only two actions, and a ability sets the stage for all the fortune that has ever been built in network marketing. It is essential to do this: think ahead and then close your eyes to millions. The famed income that is generated by the"fantastic few' ought to be earned via telephone or in person, contacting and closing distributors and potential customers-at minimum 95percent of the time that you are working in this industry.

Managers in the business are committing more and their time and money in meetings, more meetings, phone calls, motivational talks as well as listening to Dani Johnson CD, rather than making millions from one single thing crucial (that is producing sales volume through conducting prospecting, and then closing).

Blah, blah, blah, blah, blah. Did I mention that the Tuesday meeting was not the only meeting?

The New-Ninjas of MLM join their power rings in the defense of freedom. Let us explore.

What can you do within your workplace when you have to participate in frequent 'hype-a-thons', respond to requests throughout the working day, and meet all the demands and requests and demands your recesses love to dump?

Use your mobile to create an outlook! Wait until you employ someone for everything. You can throw away the course, take down your script book, then look and close your eyes to millions of new discussions one at one moment.

What do you have to say? ALL. ALL. You must take the phone seriously. It's not the way you're thinking it is. It is what they are saying. This is what they are saying. You're on your way to become a " Ninja Master' for prospection when you can hear twice as much as you talk. When you've learned to talk to someone, they will be able to join you in DROVERS.

Who should you contact? Who should you phone? Maybe start with a warm list of market opportunities, but don't get stuck. Don't be a jerk and make use of your friends script. Just be you. But, make sure you go to complete your checklist. With a list of only more than 2,000 people, it should not take more than five working days in contact with the entire company, and you can plan to contact new prospects in the shortest time possible. Pick up the phone and make several calls. Engage with people and be sincere.

How do you plan to educate your staff? Simply mention, "watch and do what you observe my actions." This will benefit you in three ways. First, your employees are trained in a way that any meeting cannot accomplish. Additionally, they will be aware that all the work your business has to do is build relationships with customers, and to close distributors to your actions. The third reason is that you avoid the effort to attend the meeting only to become bored for 2 hours. Have a blast instead of attending a meeting!

Here are seven tips that will make you incredible 1. To make millions of sales and close in this field You should be talking at least 30 people daily. This doesn't mean you are having 30 long conversations every day; it's about ensuring that your business is able to be viewed by minimum 30 people a every day, all five days of the week.

2. Don't sitdown, you're on the line. Don't babysit your downline. It's your job to do this on your own (trust my experience). If you really want to become a sponsor who is a babysitter for your employees and make you much money, and it's true. If you're seeking the convenience of time, become a person who isn't going to spend the hours and hours of their lives chasing your every need. Make sure you respond clearly to questions like "what is my plan" and encourage your group to listen to your voice and introduce new people to you.

3. Do it part-time, only five hours per day (6-7 in the case of being insane and are working already) and then turn off your weekends.

Have a break every now and then as well. If you are working in full-time employment, you aren't required to work more than three hours per day or get exhausted. You can replace your salary with a higher one by doubling it, and then you are able to quit work and start full-time work and only after that.

4. Utilize software to make the most of your resources. Telephone technology can be used to communicate with about 15 people each hour. If you've ever used your phone prior to this, you're aware of the craziness of it. It's not just accessible to a single client, but also a proper application and system understanding. You can accomplish things that a non-up-to-date user could not accomplish in 10 hours using the right system.

5. Don't invest in leads that cost a lot of dollars. If you purchase leads, you should never spend more than $1 per lead. The average cost is $8. is directly from leads cost, which is $0.50 to $0.50 or lower. However, here's an alternative to Stop wasting cash, since most leads are a waste of time. Are you looking for interested buyers? Start by reading the newspaper and begin calling

people who post classified ads and offer items for sale. Call a few Realtors. Make contact with the other Realtors. I recently made 50 hot leads and interested leads through smart use of technology, in under 30 minutes. Learn some techniques, practice it repeatedly, and when you make billions it will also save you thousands of dollars.

6. Pay attention to the people around you, really. It is important to be aware and have questions. You'll be more than simply opening your eyes, and putting your finger on your mouth. Make notes. Notes. You'll be amazed by what people will tell you when you reflect on them, but it is important to pay attention carefully.

7. These are some numbers you need to know who are a fan-cruncher Out of 30 people, 20 will admit they're willing to look at their actions. Of these, you'll get 10-value interactions and will have conversations with around three people at a basic level. If you're competent in 2/3 of them are able to be hired and you should be able to attract at the very least one.

If you have a strong work habit for a regular period of time you could find up to 500 or 300 people throughout the year, for 20 to 30 hours of work per week. The company with which you work for doesn't matter.

If you adopt this approach What will happen to you? You will be able to stay clear of a plethora of meetings and training and focus on the primary task to do for the entire group of distributors with thousands: recruiting.

With the right guidance with the right coaching, millions of dollars in income can be earned through part-time work.

I'm heading to the phone I'm off to the phone, enough talk! It's enough! Can I see you on Hawaii beaches?

Chapter 9: Network Marketing And The End

Of Stealth Prospecting

I've been working with traditional and network marketing for a number of years. Many marketing networks provide legit business prospects. You can substitute your own profits with the legitimate marketing opportunities from the network. People individuals, people, and even people are the primary source for a successful marketing company. Similar to any other business it is essential to have an ongoing flow of members joining your. In the present, you have more employees than you take on or you grow older or you've got more people than you leave and you drop or, worse and you have the same amount of people who leave in which case you slow down.

With that said how come there are there so many failures? The data indicate that the rate of failure is about 97 percent. The 3 percent who have something that the rest of us do not.

Many of the modern-day network marketing companies have a"faddish" but tokenistic presence on the internet. They are not aware of the immense potential of social media's online resources. It's not required that they "be active." We are aware that being it is not enough to get cash at the register. It requires a lot of effort to get you leads.

The strategies used to hire downline players remain the traditional way of scouring the aisles of shops and soccer games in which people who are extremely interested meet but do not possess any bone in their business. What is the point of a fantastic product, great idea and a traditional method to attract new customers?

Indeed, it is possible to connect with prospects and transform them into a downline using this strategy. However, what is "quality" of this type of prospect is always at stake. The success of network marketing relies greatly on the potential as well as the "potential" for the prospective recruit. A lot of failures and disappointments are the result of recruiting people who did not have the motivation to join in the first instance. Each prospect who loses next time is a lot harder to attract.

Thus, it is a question of whether the method that research is improved conducted and whether the prospects can be enhanced throughout the entire process. Are you looking for stealthy ways to profit from your time to build your company's most crucial source of raw materials? A lot of MLM opportunities promote stealthy prospecting in order to promote the notion that running a business is easy to set up and anyone has the ability to participate. It doesn't consider the fact that there are a few million people around the world who browse the internet and search for new opportunities and start-ups. What did you think if you had an opportunity to put yourself ahead of those searching?

Social media today offers a wealth of opportunities for network participation. Social networking or the promotion of authorizations can simplify the process of networking and lessen the threat of stealth. If your potential customers expressed an interest in your offer through an "informative" instead of a "curious" perspective What if your strategy and approach differ? The prospective client, in many cases, will be able to feel the person is you and the things you do , without the pressure of deciding immediately when you're ready to get involved. However, stealth prospects are not able to allow your prospects to act this way because they basically require that you meet, ask some questions, find an appointment, and tell them "you are calling to discuss about an opportunity you should not pass up," and hope that you'll still be interested when you contact them.

I've been in the field for several years and have networking marketing experience. The majority of marketing networks offer legit business opportunity. When you join an authentic network marketing opportunity you have the chance to supplement one's income. People are people, people, and more people are the most valuable resource to build a successful network marketing company. As with any business that you run, you require a consistent flow of new members to join your business. You either have a lot more new members, as well as more quitting than joining and in this case, you're experiencing the same amount of people who leave as you've joined and in that case, you are stagnant.

In that light how come there are the failure rates so high? Statistics reveal that the failure rate is about 97 percent. Three percent of people know something the majority of people don't.

A lot of modern network marketing firms simply have an online presence, but in a "tokenish" manner. They do not realize the immense potential of social media's online resources. It's not necessary that they "be on the internet." We all know that being online isn't necessary to use your cash counter. It is a team effort to attract your clients.

The methods used to recruit down lines traditional methods of scavenging on the streets of shops and during soccer matches, you will are met with attractive individuals who might not have any entrepreneurial bone. What's the point of a good product, new ideas however, a conventional method of attracting new development?

It is possible to use this method and turn a potential buyer into an downstream. However, it is important to note that the "price" of the prospect is always a risk. The success of network marketing is largely on the ability or preparation of the candidate. A lot of failure and discontent is the issue of recruiting individuals who have no any reason to join the organization. Every person who is not successful the second time is more difficult to find.

This raises the issue about whether the purpose of prospecting could be improved , and if prospects could become better throughout the whole process. Are stealth prospects a wise method to expand your company's most crucial resource? Many MLM incentives encourage stealthy potential to prove that running a business isn't difficult, and anyone can get it. It is a lie that ignores an enormous number of individuals all over the world use the internet to find jobs and to start their own companies. What if you could have access to being placed before the people who search?

Social networks today offer a wide range of opportunities for network participation. License marketing or social networking can make networking easier and ease the tension to stealth. If your prospective customers expressed interest in the opportunity through an informed rather than a'curious viewpoint What if your perspective and approach differ?

Outlooks can be used to allow more people to establish your personality and the things you do, without being forced to make a decision immediately if you'd like to be a part of. Stealth prospecting however doesn't permit the prospect to accomplish that since it demands that you meet, ask a few questions, contact them and tell them, "It is a good occasion to reach to discuss your business" and hope that they're intrigued when you phone them.

Let's be honest about it. Let's be honest about it. Isn't it awkward to employees of a company that you didn't know to be stranded in a store that you don't know and without a CV? What would the situation be if you were to submit an opportunity to present a business plan and required the money you invested? Doesn't this change the whole discussion?

If you're in having this outlook shopping, or whatever you're at, you've got more questions than you can answer. If you're interested, or not at all interested right away. Contrary to the casual conversation you've had it's not connected enough to the idea that this is an attainable possibility and you are able to take it on. You also wonder what it is to attract foreigners.

Social media has greatly broadened the network spectrum. The major difference is that "in-will" users are the same for both social networks. In the first few days of joining the network you can watch the list grow to a degree that requires time and also travels by secretly prospecting. Business professionals who are successful also have a network. Effective networking is about creating relationships, trust, and friendships that last. In reality, they understand that, first, and later, people will be drawn to your profile. Prospecting with stealth appears to start be attractive, then the person is drawn to the concept. It's difficult to make your prospective client a positive first impression, especially if your cheerful personality is ruined by an impressive business proposal. Based on these bases, successful firms are created. With the advent of online networks, you're able to slow the process of seeking out opportunities and let people get to know you and eliminate people who might not be interested in joining your networking marketing or business opportunities, but wish to be a resource. By using stealth marketing, your potential customer is either drawn to you immediately or deterred with your sly tactics, so that you can inquire about who and what products you offer are legal or not. It's not about old or new. It's about how you go about it. Particularly when your jolly personality is rewarded by a stunning business proposal. These are the foundations upon which good businesses are built. Through online networks, you're able to manage your pursuit and let people be aware of you, and eliminate people who might not be interested in joining your networking marketing or business opportunities but wish to remain an option. With stealth marketing, the potential customer is either drawn to you immediately or is turned off by your sneaky strategies, so you can ask whether the product you are selling is legal or not. It's not a matter of old versus new. It's dependent on how you approach it.

Money Making Internet Business Ideas for Businesses

Affiliate Marketing

Affiliate Marketing is among the fastest and most simple methods to create an online income stream. It's as easy to sign up, and then registering the services or products to the broker for business. Registration is provided by the majority of distributors. Once a sale has been made the commission is due to you. It is possible to start a web business without having to create products of your own. It is not necessary to handle payments or customer service since all information is handled by an affiliate dealer.

Your sole responsibility is to market a product or service. A lot of affiliate sellers will provide you with leads without needing the ability to market them. If you think it's simple, it's because it really is. You can make your own website to market merchandise from a merchant or put up commercial ads using pay-per click techniques for advertising. Utilizing online marketing strategies such as writing ups and marketing as well as email marketing can boost your chances of success by a significant amount.

Internet Auctions

Take a look around your house. We all have plenty of belongings that we do not wish to toss away however, we don't are using these items in attics, garages or closets. I'm betting that some of these items may even have prices! Make money from these items. Sign up for an account on eBay is cost-free and you don't need to build a website to sell your eBay products. When the item is sold, eBay takes a fee from the sale. eBay isn't just the one site that auctions online, but it's the most well-known.

Digital cameras are all that you require to take photos, but you have to manage the delivery of items to your clients. Once you have mastered selling items at home You can look for additional items to offer in locations like garage sales or discount retail stores. Wholesalers can also be contacted to inquire about a variety of items available for sale.

Sell Your Products

The products from Your Own Product Information are straightforward to buy online. How to To are a popular topic. Are you aware of what other people could benefit from something? The benefits of making your own data products is that the cost to develop them is low, there isn't any storage space required and you don't have anything to send as they are downloaded instantly. Also, you can reap some of the highest return on data items because all of the profit is kept. Even those who aren't authors will be successful in the creation and sale of their own information products. I'm pretty sure you've got some information worth sharing with another person.

You could also create your own brand to promote online sales. You are an artist that likes creating works of art? Do you have a knack for crafting? You enjoy making handmade items like candles, soap cakes, sackcloth, or a sackcloth. The list is endless as there are endless possibilities. Develop your personal website that sells your unique products. It is also possible to contact distributors and wholesalers. You can also develop an online store that sells the products you buy from the market.

Websites that are turnkey

Cost savings and time are the primary advantages of turning your website into a turnkey site. Turnkey websites are ready-to-use sites which allow you to skip the design stage of the site and proceed directly into the marketing process. It is possible to begin placing orders on a genuine turnkey website immediately following the purchase. The definitions of the most popular turnkey websites are AdSense or partner web sites. All of them have been pre-loaded with product as well as content. The turnkey websites are different in that you must have questions regarding what the turnkey site has prior to purchasing.

Sell the Services

What kinds of expertise would you offer to others? You could also be an agent for service. Hosting companies, for example generally offer reseller accounts, and some will even provide you with an online site, meaning you don't need to create your own.

Content Website

An easy and enjoyable method to earn money online is to create a website or blog on a subject that you enjoy. You can add a wealth of relevant and useful content to draw visitors to the subject. It is important to choose a subject that you already have an interest in or would like to learn more about. Once you've built your blog or website, you are able to incorporate Google AdSense to it and offer additional products that are related to your area of expertise. The focus is on the free construction of traffic writing up advertising content and reputation links will enable users to make profit greater.

Websites for Members

In lieu of constructing your own website and providing your valuable data for free You can also develop an association platform to market your content efficiently. This is a profitable alternative, even though instead of selling one item at each time, you earn income from recurring memberships. This method requires more effort however it definitely is worth it in the end. The public is willing to purchase memberships for online content the same way as they would pay for memberships paid for newspapers, magazines and other clubs. Exclusive content can be provided like content, exclusive resources, such as coaching or mentoring as well as items such as books, apps or even music.

There are numerous ways to earn money online. The ideas discussed here have resulted in a large amount of revenue for many. One of the most crucial things you could do now is simply pick a topic. It is possible to start with a particular type of online business, then switch to a different type of business. If you are looking to have more than one site it is not necessary limit yourself to only one type. You'll gain more knowledge, improve in your knowledge, gain more experience and earn more. The most successful companies on the internet are simply ordinary individuals who have made the decision to go online.

Businesses use Remote Desktop Services with QuickBooks

Remote Desktop Services (RDS) can offer a variety of advantages and help your organization to improve the efficiency of their Quick books Enterprise Solutions technology performance and quality.

1. It simplifies RDS IT services to simplify QuickBooks installation and maintenance requirements. In the beginning administrators of systems can swiftly grant users access to their QuickBooks accounts by installing it onto the RDS server and establishing them immediately.

Additional software updates can only be run on a single computer. The advantage lies in the fact that Microsoft and third-party developers provide Remote Desktop Communication client software that works with the majority of OS which includes Mac, Linux and older versions of Windows.

This means that organizations can cut costs in their infrastructure for IT since the computer hardware and software don't have to be upgraded or changed frequently.

External software like Adobe Acrobat Reader and Microsoft Excel can be installed in the same database to ensure that users can connect to other applications they would like while using QuickBooks.

2. QuickBooks that is running on a network and using RDS can beat those who don't. It's more speedy and efficient. If you are in a network that does not utilize RDS, QuickBooks data companies will be on a separate workstation or file server typically referred to the database server.

To access their company database, the system that the user operates their QuickBooks should have a copy QuickBooks application installed . It must also connect with the server for database.

The work with QuickBooks files on all systems needs to transfer to the server for database from the computer in order to integrate it into the file containing the data.

If one system or link is not performing as it should processing time will be delayed for all, and the server will be in the process of waiting for commands that are entered by the various systems in the link to get processed.

In this particular aspect of the setup the computer with the least power or most slow connection will force the network to speed up. Once the network is set up using RDS and the QuickBooks application and the company's data file that are both saved in the servers, there is no backup of the QuickBooks program is necessary on each computer of the user.

Users sign in directly to the database, which executes an QuickBooks request and runs the commands. The volume of data transferred via the network is minimal since only keystrokes and movement of the mouse are needed by the user's computer.

The slowest speed at which communication occurs in the system is no longer a matter of debate since activities are centrally measured

, allowing everyone to work at their own speed.

Since the information is always in your database system, that work will not be lost even in the event that the connection gets cut during the time a client is working within QuickBooks through RDS.

3. A more efficient and less expensive RDS lets QuickBooks customers to operate from their home office, workstation as a satellite office or anyplace. Remote access alternatives offer various features, however users are still unable to use it effectively.

Contrary to the RDS needs a significantly greater quantity of data to be transmitted, which ensures that the QuickBooks performance is enhanced even in instances of low bandwidth. These remote access services generally require a specific workstation in the office to be connected to every remote client.

If a computer is accessible via a distance, no one other than the employee can access the computer. Fortunately, RDS would allow QuickBooks remote access to several employees through the shared database, ensuring that the workstations do not need to be connected.

4. Increased security for financial information security is crucial for every business. With the use of QuickBooks Enterprise Solutions, RDS provides the business with additional security. In the beginning, administrators of the system must grant each user has access to the different levels of database access.

The administrator of the system will decide the programs that are available to each user that is managed by the server. This means that various employees have access to the database for different purposes however, QuickBooks Enterprise Software can only be used by those who wish to utilize it.

QuickBooks administrators can also establish the application level controls to define what functions are accessible the users who use QuickBooks and what kind of access they are entitled to including creating, updating, taking away printing, or only viewing. With RDS businesses also have the ability to reduce the chance of theft or lost information.

Additionally, since the data resided on the database, laptops affected should not have duplicates of the data file of the company.

5. Further RDS regulation grants system teachers with more power over QuickBooks. The code as well as the business data file are kept in a location accessible only to administrators. Remote Desktop Services is set up in the same way, and RDS is a lot more easy for businesses to establish.

Intuit Solution Providers offer on-site assistance for customers who require assistance from a professional in securing appropriate hardware, software and setting up databases for RDS2.

They also provide expertise in the implementation and configuration of QuickBooks Business solutions. If your business has an IT department They usually have the expertise and knowledge to install RDS. Additionally, the majority of retailers selling servers also have these services available.

Chapter 10: Mid-Size Manufacturing Firms

Need More Effective Marketing

If you're a small-medium-sized distributor or service business which sells to other businesses (that is, "business to business marketers") You need to pay attention to advertising and marketing because many things have changed over the past couple of years.

Let's begin by describing "marketing" within the realm of business-to-business , before we describe the changes that have occurred.

Many business owners say that "marketing" refers to "advertising." Marketing is described as nothing could be further over the mark.

Advertising can be defined easily advertisements are published in trade magazines, newspapers, directories or on yellow pages. Maybe you send an email directly or receive an exhibit at a trade event or perhaps you're trying on the internet with banner ads, or you've sent customer data. Advertising plus publicity is publicity.

You might also think of your site in the form of "advertising," but it isn't a sign of anything, since your site isn't "targeted" towards anyone; it's just a generalization.

So, what's commercialization?

Although advertising is about advertisements, advertising is only one of the marketing ingredients like tomatoes, which is only one component of a great pasta sauce.

Associate advertisements to a football team. It is quarterback who's the most well-known (advertising) however, on defense and offense other players are part of winning teams. They are well-educated and competent.

Marketing is an assortment of components that allow you to grow and market your brand and services, maintain customers and grow your market share.

Take a look: If your team members - for instance management, technology, distribution, product development parts, customer service and operations-are all individually involved (which is the case with small and medium-sized manufacturing companies is quite common) They are all team members with no captain (marketing)- and the team members are affected by the brand's image as well as market share or lead generation.

Marketing is, simply the discipline that brings all things together. Advertising is a discipline in its strict sense.

Marketing Expert Business-to-business marketers whether small or large employ a marketing director who will ensure that their comprehensive marketing strategies incorporate advertising, sales, management customer service, as well as after-sales services.

But, many businesses cannot pay for an entire time marketing manager. A marketing advertising agency is involved here, or at least a consultant, who can help you in designing a marketing/advertising/ communications strategy.

Change later, advertising talent recruitment... However, now we are back to "what is changing in the field of marketing and advertising business-to-business industry" over the last couple of years. A number, yes that is dominated by being the Internet.

The Internet has transformed the method of doing business. We refer to buyers and sellers through "we."

Buyers look at their data differently than they did years ago, from business publications and directories, to online searches. They can also select their peers ' reviews on social media sites.

The sellers have also altered how they market their products. This ranges in telemarketing, cold call and direct mail, to web pages "optimized" specifically for search engines (SEOs) and pay-per click ads, online media and helpful "how-to" documents available for download, and many more.

The Internet has produced a myriad of techniques and tools that allow businesses to sell its products quicker and more effectively that "traditional" methods like commercial advertising traditional press releases and direct mail, all at significantly less expense.

These tools aren't only cheaper; they also help to make marketing more quantifiable.

For instance marketing via email, which is an important tool for launch of new products as well as customer retention and constant customer relationships and the creation of brand is not just cost-effective but additionally equipped with real-time analysisthat lets you know the way your email or e-news campaigns are performing.

Analytics on your website, many of which are free, help you not only to continuously analyze the number of visits to your site (both new and existing users) as well as the most important things about them, including how they move around and how long they stay on various websites, and even the last page they left.

It will cost you approximately the same amount to distribute your announcement to a crowd of tens of thousands of prospects , as an all-new toner cartridge.

Marketing professionals often overlook the importance of web SEO (or SEO) but it's something that should be an essential part of your marketing strategy. Your site doesn't require the expense of a whole It's possible that you don't need an entirely new (and costly) layout. It could be necessary to update your content and ensure that it is in line with the search engine's algorithms. their constantly changing algorithmic changes.

The strategy is crucial. You must first have an outline, a precise marketing strategy that outlines the goals of your business and branding and targets for market share as well as the strategies that aid you in achieving these goals and the strategies which show how your plans are put into practice. You'll also require an appropriate budget. A strategic plan can help you achieve your goals If it's executed correctly.

Find an expert to help you make this happen Someone who is familiar with the modern business-to-business landscape. Make sure you have the support of management, marketing customer service, management, and other team members since they are all on the same page.

Add them to your strategy and plan for selling through agents, dealers, or distributors. Connect to them and then drive them to sales.

Be sure to define what makes you different and your USP or your particular offer (sometimes called your value-proposition) to let your potential customers know what differentiates you from the competition.

Make sure that the entire team is receiving the identical message. The importance of messaging is element of branding process and delivering what is called the "product promises."

It is possible to reconsider how you present yourself as part your branding strategy, but it will be costly and time-consuming when it is the right strategy is used.

It's the Advertising Action Plan: a highly profitable investment. Then execute your plan. A sound marketing plan that is that is based on a thorough analysis of the market and a strategic roadmap along with timeframes, budgets, and timelines is one of the best investment options.

These are the most common strategies for marketing that include press advertisements, banner ads online or pay-per click notifications E-news or e-marketing, customer support, search engine enhancements dealer support, or social media.

It could be an internal company or marketing agency or even a mix of both.

The budget for marketing media is okay It's a subject which is subject to change. Additionally, the most important thing is the marketing strategy that outlines the steps you have to take to make sure that your plan is covered.

A well-planned plan will outline the strategies (tasks). If you employ the task budget method they are each costing and your budget outline will be in place. If you'd like to modify the budget, but stay within the budget, you can change the amount or frequency of your tasks such as your objectives strategies, strategies, and tactics.

Most small and medium businesses use a percentage of their sales-marketing-advertising budget as a guide; this typically accounts for between 0.5% and 3.0% of their revenue to the size of the company. For example, a business with 10 million dollars of sales would need to budget at 2% or 200 dollars, and a business that has 100 million dollars should budget 5percent of the budget, or 500 000 dollars. Keep in mind that this budget will apply not just to advertising, but also to the whole marketing mix that includes manufacturing, press web-based work, as well as the costs paid to your business or to a consultant.

However, the goal-to-tactic budgeting approach is always more accurate than an % of sales because they are based upon your competition environment, brand's objectives and, more likely it is the reality that a lot of the essential marketing tasks you've left unfinished must be completed.

The next step is to find someone who has experience in marketing and out of business, and includes new, e-based techniques. Find consensus regarding how to implement the (written) strategies for advertising. Create and stick to the budget. Apply the plan effectively and thoroughly. Also, track your results so that you can track the progress over time and calculate the return on investment from your marketing expenditures.

Small Business Marketing From Start to Start

"Perhaps the beginning line could be your final line. Be prepared to go back." Writer: Tablo It is common to lay out the goals and define the tasks needed to reach the desired goal when discussing a task. Consider something as simple as building a home. The buyers and the designers determine the exact dimensions of the home's "footprint"-the quantity and the dimensions of bathrooms, bedrooms and kitchen designs. It is an obligation of the builder to design the plans that are presented for approval by the city or local authority. Once the approval is granted, the builder assigns an administrator to carry out the necessary steps.

So, when all parties operate in reverse order small-scale business advertising is the best. The consumer (the external marketing director or external decision maker) has to look at where they would like to get there. As opposed to the construction of a house there are a myriad of ways to define the success.

In this case, performance can be defined as an increase in income from the current rate to a higher rate. Let's say, for instance, we imagine that the company has increased its revenues by 10 % per year in the past five years. The marketing goal is to increase the growth rate to 20 percent per year in a reasonable time.

A brand new product, a service, or a brand new solution that has a better ROI than previous launches previously, can be launched successfully.

Marketing is now working towards these goals since there's no better word than reverse. Marketing specialists begin with the final phase, setting one or more goals to be achieved. Marketing analyzes the different components of these phases in a thorough way, just like managing projects. But, the strategies used to promote (also called"the promotion mix) may have different costs and various options will require more or less time to implement the task.

Here's an example of the method and approach to market small businesses.

Let's move forward with a goal to increase revenues by 20% over within the next 18-24 month period.

Why isn't a business date set? It's foolish to set an untimely date with an ever-changing variety of marketing tools as well as common formats. Imagine completing a project prior to when Facebook, Twitter, and LinkedIn started. It is likely for these "new" methods of communication with influencers and consumers can significantly impact the time frame for completion.

A well-designed website is more effective however it must be a live tool that is able to adapt to changes in the way people seek information. A well-designed website is sufficient if it offers only basic information about the business, the product and its brand as well as the solution and the best place to find details.

The landing pages need to be clear and simple (and non-technical.) The landing page(s) should be on the site. If someone is searching and comes across your advertisement (more on it in the future) the landing page is the place where you click to take the link directly to a particular page. So, they can't look up the management history office locations,

You must visit the site page, which will address the subject using the keyword(s) you were searching for as well as your "bait" in the ad that you press the link. Most people are smart enough to browse the site on their own , if they're interested in learning more about the company. The purpose of this page is to fulfill the SPECIFIC needs and SPECIFIC solution that brought them to that page.

Okay. OK. Imagine we have this solid landing page (presumably numerous for each solution or product that is being executed). When did people come? Where did you look for yours among the millions of pages of universes?

The word magic stands for CONTENT.

Content shouldn't be confused as advertising. Evidently, marketing through content is swiftly recognized as such and harms the product. Content provides education. It offers opinions, stories ideas, accomplishments, and concepts and is free of the expectation of earning a profit that is more than the recognition that the writer is an expert in the field as well as willing with no an ulterior motive to give facts. This is the altruistic motive that customers want beyond clever jingles surveys, puzzles, or quizzes.

Consider your competitors. Let's step back. Which competitors are they who are they, and how do they have to say or sell, say or even suggest that they intend to place their products in a less favorable light than yours regardless of whether they are real or not? The arguments (real or not) are frequently ignored simply because they're produced by costly research companies whose lipsticks are more attractive than the pigs wearing them.

Find out who your rivals were at the time. Are they really able to create something superior to yours, or just done enough to make consumers believe that you're the latest news the day before? With more than 25 years of expertise in IT marketing and sales Some companies seem to be unable to replicate this, Digital Equipment, etc. was either destroyed or absorbed by other companies. When other innovators came along and re-invented these companies, they eventually settled down during the beginning of computers. It's not necessary to think back to 20 decades ago of Myspace, Zune, and even Napster.

Make the effort to analyze your competitors and develop an honest, simple SWOT (S= Strengths and weaknesses, T-Threats, Opportunities) analysis so that you can pinpoint the weaknesses and target them in your marketing strategies.

The most significant system an organization can use for advertising is the server. The server (whether within top-of-the line CRM systems or an the form of a great table). Apart from former and current clients, it must be regularly monitored, fed, reviewed and manipulated, and not less efficient for every other dollar or hour. The server does not just contain contacts, but also a record of bad and good business interactions. It's also the first step to identify possible customers with genuine and suspected "warts," and to have a discussion with these issues prior to launching campaigns.

We have all the elements and all the steps to guide customers or influencer(s) on to the appropriate landing page(s) which is where we can start a dialogue and begin clicking on customers. Cover all the nuances of email marketing and snail mail marketing. blog content marketing, as well as social media distribution like Twitter, Facebook, LinkedIn as well as (in specifically) Google+. Connect your budget via Google AdWords and follow up with industry events at which experts in the field are seeking to share their ideas and knowledge.

Summary: Similar steps can be implemented for smaller companies that do not require a huge budget nor a dedicated workforce. Instead, a professional in marketing who is a good fit for the company and is an expert in measuring efficiency, could improve the business's performance, and assist reach both long-term and short-term goals by working with digital partners. Make the effort to analyze your competition and create an honest, simple SWOT (S= Strengths and Weaknesses; O= Opportunities O= Opportunities Threats to the Organization) analysis so that you can pinpoint the weaknesses and address these in your marketing campaigns.

The primary device an organization can utilize to advertise is the server. The server (whether within an innovative CRM program or an a table that is excellent). In addition to current and/or past customers, it needs to be regularly updated, reviewed, analyzed and manipulated, and not sub-optimized to make any other dollar or hour. The server is not just a repository of contacts, but also a record of both good and bad client interactions. It is also the first step to identify prospective customers with genuine as well as suspected "warts," and to have a discussion with these issues prior to launching campaigns.

We have the complete set of pieces and the actions to guide customers or influencer(s) towards the destination page(s) and from there we can begin a conversation and get them to click on our customers. Cover all the nuances of email marketing as well as snail mail marketing. blogging content marketing, and social media distribution, such as Twitter, Facebook, LinkedIn as well as (in particularly) Google+. Connect your budget through Google AdWords and follow up on industry-related events where experts from the field are pursuing to share their ideas and knowledge.

Summary: Similar steps can be used for small businesses that do not require a huge budget nor a dedicated workforce. A marketing professional who is a good fit for the company, and is skilled in measuring effectiveness, can improve the business's performance, and assist to achieve both long-term and short-term objectives as an online partner.

Boost Your Visual Marketing Strategy

Certain advertisers are aware that creating visual images does not fit their needs.

Good news? The best part? Creativity is now mastered, and you don't have to fight by using visual ads.

Are you looking to improve your social media strategy by using more visually appealing content? Visual advertising is more than just a simple quote from Google and re-posting.

You might even be thinking what you can do to make appealing and attractive a image that is shared? What kind of image do people are eager to discuss or share with followers?

There are a lot of reports and articles on the process by which visual marketing images are made. But, this information can take weeks to develop and then applied to your business.

We did the work for you. This chapter offers suggestions on how to make visually appealing content.

According to the Content Marketing Institute estimated that 70 percent of marketers produce more visually-oriented content.

Consider, can you create adequate visual media? If not, it could be because the concept of 'project is intimidating to you. Don't worry about it and these suggestions can assist you.

This chapter will provide numerous tips to assist you in creating more visually appealing content. This will help your message stick to people who search on the internet by utilizing these strategies.

The creation of visually appealing content is the top priority on lists of marketers and should be yours too. (Social Mediaexaminer.com) Infographic and visual sensitivity are beneficial to your target audience. Are you using these strategies to communicate with your customers?

The usage of video ads was up by 8% during 2014, and the use of infographics increased by nine percent. If you are a business owner who is based at home you'll be able to dedicate more time and energy in the production of visual content. The majority of the increase in engagements are due to Facebook posts that contain images or videos. (Source: EMarketer.com) What is this all about? Facebook users are seeking than just blatant calls to action to buy products. Your posts should be a source of inspiration, to communicate with your audience, and not use excessive text. It is time to move to visual advertising if your posts are filled with text. You can now include photos and videos in your posts.

What makes a social media image acceptable for sharing? Why should we consider sharing our images? Good questions. Good questions. You've been receiving free marketing each when someone is sharing your photo. Your message is visible to the world. By limiting your message, you get more done!

Let's examine what is it that makes a photo on social media to be shared: 1. Emotion: They'll share it when they feel the emotion.

2. Relevance Image and target audience will be a good fit.

3. Colors: Select the right colors that match the look of your followers to gain more shares.

4. Typography: Pick fonts that look nice and work well together. Choose fonts that your target audience will be able to understand.

5. Select the appropriate words to inspire your audience to engage.

The best method to improve the quality of content on social media is via pictures and images. Focus on creating visually appealing content that draws your audience to join a marketing funnel. In the end you'll find specific information that will help distinguish the customers from the visitors.

Professional buyers will always want more information throughout their lives. They will want cases studies, webinars and write-ups (or white paper). To access the data behind visual content will open the way to buyers who are serious.

Tip #1 Titles are an element of your visual content. It is the basis for your images' titles. You'd like them to be out! You would like them to go!

Let's consider a few things to help you select the most appropriate titles for your digital marketing.

1. We live in an age of scrolling at a record rate on their social networks. A catchy title can discern your content from the "noise" of news feeds.

2. Your image only has one second to catch the attention of your viewers. However, your caption (or primary goal in the photo) should also be able to speak to the viewers.

3. If the image is appealing to your target audience Make sure the title is longer. If your

title is too not long enough, people won't click on the call to action and then scroll to the next item.

4. The most important information to help you solve your issue is your background information. The title must be clear and concise and offer an the answer to your query.

The title of your picture is everywhere. It is therefore important to choose a photo with a clear and concise title that can be seen across a variety of places. If you are creating text-based content, you must make sure that the different versions will be displayed as "name solely." This is a form of visual advertising, your only chance to get the focus of your target audience.

Tip #2 Color Psychology of colors used in visual advertisements A discussion on the role of color in appealing to the buyer is a common practice for a long time.

A well-known and high-end coffee retailer is a fantastic illustration of today's color-based marketing. The primary color they use for marketing is green. Green is a color that customers associate with. is connected to relaxation and wealth when you look at the color chart.

Do you think that the marketing of this cafe is true? They invite people to stop in and relax with 5-8 dollars worth of coffee. A lot of people say that without a visit this cafe and they won't be able to start their day. It's quite clever, isn't it?

Studies have shown that different colors impact the buying decision of a buyer. Over the years marketing departments have relied on this data. Consider the power of colors and make your marketing decisions with a sense of purpose.

According to an B2B survey, 83 percent of people say the color of an advertisement can influence their decision to buy.

It is important to note that color alone will make anyone purchase or not buy. However, color can affect the product and the marketing when it is done right. Also, how long customers spend to learn about your product.

How can you make use of this to improve your strategy for visual marketing?

Start with a particular topic of color. The appropriate color is determined by what demographics you have for your target audience as well as your message. The next step is to choose your social media profiles to ensure you have the right shape, text, font and images.

What are the effects of colors on the way you shop?

A variety of factors affect what consumers decide to purchase. However, the majority of their purchases are based on visual clues like the color. The color you choose is crucial to reinforce the message of your post. Always refer to a color chart in order to ensure that the color you choose will help your post. Thus, you would like your clients to take action.

You may think your font is just a style choice. The truth is that the font is your body language. It can communicate to readers the reader a lot, without you even knowing it. Different fonts determine the length of time you spend reading your article.

The previous guidelines discussed the importance of embracing and sharing your images. Did you know that the font you choose will impact the amount of shares (attention)? How? How? Let's look. Let's look.

Different fonts can create different feelings.

Fonts will encourage readers to complete the task they wish to take.To encourage them to share the actions they're taking? Think about the message you're transmitting and the emotions you wish to evoke from your readers.

Three steps are required in choosing your preferred font. Make sure the font you select will enhance or weaken the text.

Be sure to look beyond the words you've written while creating the visual representations. A quote can be a great illustration here. The goal is to choose the font that best matches what you want to convey in the text. It is important to think outside the lines you wrote. The sound may be complicated however, it's not.

3 Stages: 1. Make a decision about your feelings Are you a pleasant kind of person? Are you, as an agency more serious? You can be jolly and easy to get around, or you can be

serious and tough. But, mixing them does not always result in a cohesive message.

2. Pick three different versions of fonts: select three fonts that best fit the brand's image. Then, create your visual image using three different fonts. Leave the task and come back after a while. If you've got 'fresh eyes, you'll be able to instantly determine which font will suit your message the best.

3. There's nothing more frustrating than a text cannot be read. Perhaps You yourself were a victim? You are seeing the attempt of visual advertising however the text can't be understood due to it was the wrong font selection. Simply because you think the font looks pretty but the viewer is unable to comprehend the font. What we've learned in the last two lessons If your audience isn't digesting the message in a timely manner it will take them longer to process the information.

A study by Trend Reports showed that 65% to 85% of people declare themselves to be visually-oriented students. Visual learners prefer to focus and study rather than read and comprehend. Marketers must improve their image quality to meet the needs of most visual learners.

Great for visual learners. You can differentiate yourself from competitors who only use text. If you decide to tie pictures to your colors titles, and fonts it is important to keep the importance of these elements. Do the images you select fit the target audience for which you select it?

Vision learners interpret information by using the part of their brain that is related to vision brain. This is sixty times more efficient than portion that processes written information.

Visual students examine the image and decide if it is what they want and so on. The brain is the part of your brain which will tell you to stop, study or make a move because something is not the way to go.

There are three questions you should ask yourself: Brand"Viewer Niche" Important news feed update If you say yes, the next step is to guide the viewer away from your image and to your call to action. Yes. The main goal is to convince your audience members to take the specified step.

When you design each image it is important to consider, "Does my audience make sense?" Not sure if your audience's best interaction? Take a look at the leaders in the field. What will your marketing visual strategy appear? Find posts that are getting lots of engagement and discover a winning mix to suit your needs.

Attract the attention of your viewers Most people in this digital time are overwhelmed. When we interact with the vast majority of people in our lives all the information we receive is overwhelming. So, the majority of people on social media are quick to scan and skim. The most important thing to do with advertising that is visual is to make sure you have readers and scanners to scan at the content and not the other. A lot of tourists are bored in reading publications via social media. We need pictures that get their attention.

Tip #5 Use Instagram's more Like filters. You can alter your photos using more than 12 filters. The days of selecting an option to filter out your photo appeared better. Now, you can select the most scientifically-based filter to boost the performance of your picture. The reason why is that we study visual advertising isn't it?

When you snap a photograph you can alter it in the following ways with filters.

1. Click the filter that you'd like to apply.

2. Repeat the filter in case you wish to alter the force filtered by moving the slider upwards or downwards. To save your changes simply press the Check.

3. Tap Next to include a caption for the photo and the location.

Filters can make your photos appear more sophisticated. Study studies that you select show more thought or comments and even actions as well as the editing results.

We used filters to make our content look better. We are now aware of how our content is boosted through filters. So , what are you able to choose to use Instagram filters? There are two choices to enhance your photos without Instagram.

1. Wix Photo Editor If you are using Wix the photo editor can be used to alter your photos.

The photo editor of Wix allows you to improve your photos when working on your website. Instagram's image editor competes with Wix's with the ease and variety.

2. If you browse the internet and browse the internet, you'll find many image editors are accessible. These programs give you total control over how you take a look at what you end up with as your image.

Befunky* Canva* Ribbet These are trusted photo editors, which are all available online and, for the most part free or at a affordable cost.

Tips #3, Graphs 1. Graphs 1. How do you use Visual Advertising Quotes Where do you fit in the social media timeline? Do you prefer using social media to meet new people and build friendships?

Are you part of the generation who loves quotes of children with smiles or hilarious memes?

There's no problem with any group within which you are a part when you utilize social media for your personal time.

If you're looking to establish your brand using cats or memes There is something missing.

You cannot afford as a visual marketing professional to waste all the time you spend on social networks. If your photos do not reflect your brand message, you're not doing well in your business.

Sure there is a way to grow your child meme by gaining shares, likes, and even comments. However, ask yourself "My customers want the product?"

Let's take a look at graphic designs and how they resonate with your message to reach your goal of visual marketing.

The most satisfying part of the hour you've spent making an image. It's bizarre, cynical and you think that you're smart!

You share your thoughts on social media sites and anticipate to receive comments and queries from your business. But, the post did not pertain to your business at home. You didn't get any follow-up questions and, consequently. Perhaps a"like' or two. Sure. No single sale, but. What's wrong?

The most important question to be asking yourself is: did the investment effort match with the strategy for selling?

If your quotes do not endorse a broader contextual goal (to act), your initiative has failed. Be cautious when you create and publish visual content without understanding the reason behind why you are doing it. How each piece of content fits in your sales strategy.

2. Infographics: Use of infographics to Help you understand complex problems Do you remember tip number 4 with the right image? How did we approach your target audience of 65% to 85 percentage of students who are visual? So infographics are a huge hit. They're also very effective!

There are many aspects of your industries that have complex topics (or maybe boring ones). If you attempt to describe them to your audience via text, it's not very well received.

Make sure you create an infographic that conveys the message in a complex infographic. Now , you've made it simple to comprehend your target audience. The'visual pathways' that help your customers are highly effective pieces of infographics. The report's conclusion is a call to action to read more or do something.

The action calls take the user to a specific location, most likely your website. The goal of your infographic is to provide an image that guides your reader to take an action.

An excellent example of making an uninteresting topic interesting can be found in Distribution Map Infographics.

Here's an example of the landscapes of global economic productivity. I know, what a boring topic? If you're an economist, and I apologise for the situation!

You could also develop an infographic distribution chart using a range of colors. By using gradations of light to dark this is an effective method of displaying the boring aspects of a topic. Another approach to draw attention to this is to display information in a structured 3D format. The eye is drawn from a distance at the arrangement because of its distinctiveness.

Your purpose infographic: To illustrate abstract statistics, use color gradation.

Visual advertising is essential to reach your target audience and raise brand awareness. Implement these components to implement your visual marketing plan as you progress.

Video marketing and credibility

Have you ever thought about appearing in a film? Have you ever thought about having your own TV show? Do thousands, hundreds, or even millions of viewers are eager to be heard? If yes, then you've got the perfect video.

Video is among the most popular marketing tools in the world. It's not just for advertisements However, when it's good viewers feel like they have known you for a while, and that's a great way to market.

There are two main techniques for video that include screen capture and camera. Your colleagues, you, or experts go through a course or demonstrate to the camera, conduct a an audiobook trailer, testimonial, or interview; or make the speech. You can record your expertly conducted interview or other kind of interview , instead of recording the audio. Screen capture transforms an event into a movie on your computer, such as PowerPoint slides, or even online sites.

YouTube is the top online video platform. There are other sites but YouTube is so well-known that it's essential to upload your video. YouTube is a site to post videos that individuals can submit and share video content.

Whatever you're looking for you'll find videos on it. Millions of videos are accessible on YouTube every day. Wouldn't you like your video to be included in that number of views? Videos can be used to show off your products, create a visual and build your subscriber list. Since YouTube is the most visited video site In this chapter I'll specifically focus on YouTube. For downloading the video you are able to look up YouTube for "mechanics." Also, look up "subscribing to YouTube," "loading a video,"" "setup of an YouTube channel,"" "setup for a YouTube channel,"" "searching for an YouTube channel." If you're confident in front of cameras, it's the best method to reach your target audience. You're real and people are more connected to your message than any other news.

The more you can practice before the camera, the more comfortable you are. It's easier to record voice-overs instead of being in front of the camera, when you use screenshots. If you're not comfortable in recording voice or video you can let someone else take the picture. But make sure you do it before deciding that you're not capable of doing it. It's important to let your personality out. Make sure you are aware of the advantages of your business and market and you'll make the job more simple.

What is Your Message mean?

Four areas on which the video's focus include: Who are you?

Who is the target of the video?

What are your methods of problem-solving?

What's the solution?

If you are able to be able to answer these questions clearly the videos will benefit your viewers.

Your own channel One of the greatest things about YouTube is the ability to make your own channel available on YouTube. This lets your brand and subscribers to be boosted and is simple to follow the directions. It is possible to include your name, your account's type as well as the videos you upload, and any other information about users you input into your stream. You'll also have a subscriber database for YouTube to keep your subscribers at the top of the list of videos you upload.

The more users you have in your list of email addresses, the greater number of people are receiving your messages. You can also get more buyers to your door when you've got something you want to sell. Like other aspects of your online activity you should promote your channel actively by promoting social media, such as Facebook, Twitter, LinkedIn, and any other social media platforms you are using. Include a brief description of the URLs your channel's address is in your signature file or in your resource box.

Video SEO is among the most effective ways to achieve SEO. Make use of your title, description of the video keywords and tags within your search terms. Google recognizes these and helps improve your SEO.

Include an URL that is clickable (the beginning line is the the most crucial) on the top line in your description tag. To make your URL clickable be sure to be sure to include "Http:/www" section. Viewers are able to go directly to your blog, website or landing page from there.

If you are promoting your event, book or other product, posting videos on YouTube can result in better search engine rankings therefore, ensure that YouTube is a part of the social media advertising strategy.

Consistency is the key to maintaining a consistent stream of YouTube videos, particularly in the case of subscribers after you have added videos to your marketing plan. One reason they signed up to check out what you're up to and to learn from you and to follow your message.

Different types of video demonstrations Thumbnails Book trailers What - top is the most effective for SEO. Let's suppose you're a dog trainer for puppies. What is the best use for video clips other than to demonstrate a teaching technique? What is a better application? If you're a chef and you want to show the viewers to make use of the kitchen equipment, what better method than to use a video? If you want to teach a particular method of art videos are the right choice. You could film a brief part of a class to draw your viewers' attention and guide them to the place where they can access all the information on training. Video usage is unlimited.

Methods to promote your video. You can tweet the URL, post it on your Facebook wall, and then link the video directly to your blog using embedded software once the video is uploaded.

Conclusion

In putting decades of sales-related knowledge into this article It's your responsibility to improve your skills to the point that you are able to maximize the advantages that come from following my guidelines. Keep in mind that sales is a specific field of business in which the ability to develop your gut instincts will get you far.

Additionally, think about your opening line. If you're selling products that are unique you can use funny lines for your openings, or funny bits of humor that can be beneficial in place of the standard "Hi I'm calling from this firm, and I'm selling some new products that I believe you will find interesting". Be cautious when applying these tactics frequently because they could backfire heavily against your business.

If your company offers additional details about clients, like their the interests of them, their name, office assistant, vacation dates or other information. Utilize that information to recommend the most appropriate products from your catalog. But beware of insincere small talk at all at all. There's nothing more annoying than having to conversation with salespeople who clearly made calls with the intention of selling the product. Additionally, if you're able to make use of your creativity to deal with employees and others who act as call-screeners or gatekeepers for your clients. Just ask them their nameand inform them that you've had the opportunity to meet with them in the last time and ask the boss's schedule was full or in a tight spot in the present time, and if you need to move your appointment, or contact them again to confirm this with your client. Although this may not be the case, you can employ persistence and ingenuity to reach out to your customer. Whether or not they decide to be impressed by your skills in sales and give you a token of appreciation for their valuable time, or even if they decide to purchase the product after you've pointed it out, is entirely dependent on them.

The guiding principle, from now on must be: Never accept a no for an answer without hearing it first. It's a matter of being distinctive and standing above the rest in terms of professionalism and results at work. Therefore, you should not be content with being excellent as those who are around you.

The notion that salespeople are similar to sharks is thought of as a derogatory statement, there's nothing wrong in having the ambition and drive that a shark has, so that you don't possess the morals and ethos that come with sharks.

www.ingramcontent.com/pod-product-compliance
Lightning Source LLC
Chambersburg PA
CBHW050401120526
44590CB00015B/1784